GETTING INTO

LAW

TROTMAN

This edition published in 1994
by Trotman and Company Ltd,
12 Hill Rise, Richmond, Surrey TW10 6UA

© Trotman and Company Limited 1994

British Library Cataloguing in Publication Data
A catalogue record for this book is available from
the British Library.

ISBN 0 85660 217 5

Printed in Great Britain by Redwood Books,
Trowbridge, Wiltshire

CONTENTS

GET IN WITH A GUIDE

Getting into higher education may be the toughest challenge you've yet faced. MPW Guides can help . . .

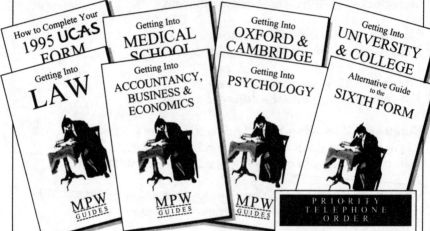

How to Complete Your 1995 **UCAS** FORM

Getting Into **MEDICAL SCHOOL**

Getting Into **OXFORD & CAMBRIDGE**

Getting Into **UNIVERSITY & COLLEGE**

Getting Into **LAW**

Getting Into **ACCOUNTANCY, BUSINESS & ECONOMICS**

Getting Into **PSYCHOLOGY**

Alternative Guide to the **SIXTH FORM**

MPW GUIDES

Getting into higher education may be the toughest challenge you've yet faced. MPW Guides can help.

Written by experts with a wealth of experience, MPW Guides are set out in straightforward language. They give clear, practical advice to help you win a place on the course of your choice. You'll find MPW Guides in all good bookshops. To get your Guides fast, phone 081-332 2132 quoting your Access or Visa number.

MPW is the UK's leading group of independent sixth form colleges. We have over twenty years experience of guiding students

through the application procedures for higher education and helping them gain the high grades they need. We cover a wide range of A-Level and GCSE subjects in courses lasting from ten weeks (retakes) to two years. At our colleges in London, Birmingham, Bristol and Cambridge, we teach in small groups or individually. MPW offers a unique blend of expert tuition, close supervision, study skills and exam technique.

If you would like more information about MPW, please telephone us on 071-835 1355.

ACKOWLEDGEMENTS

This book is the baby of a number of contributors without whose specialist knowledge it would not have been born. Our thanks go to the following:

Dr. James Holland, who co-wrote chapters 1 and 2 and Annex A, is the Associate Dean (Academic Studies) in the Faculty of Law at the University of the West of England in Bristol. He is also the co-author of *Learning Legal Rules* published by Blackstone Press.

Julian Webb also wrote chapters 1 and 2 and Annex A. He is the Director of Postgraduate Programmes in the Faculty of Law at the University of the West of England, and has co-written *Learning Legal Rules* with Dr Holland.

Alastair Boag is the author of chapters 4 and 5 of *Getting into Law*. He was educated at Harrow and Worcester College, Oxford where he read English. He then went on to be the administrator of the inner city charity 'London Youth Adventure' before joining MPW as a Personal Tutor in 1992.

Paul Whiteside has written Annex B on the British Legal System. He studied History at both University College London and Queen Mary and Westfield College before completing a Diploma in Law at City University and attending a College of Law. For the past ten years he has been teaching Law and social sciences at undergraduate and A-level. Paul teaches Law at MPW.

Joanne Hubert, who has written everything else, was educated at the Ladies' College, Guernsey and the University of Kent where she read Law. In recent years she has travelled through parts of Asia and worked in Australia and Japan teaching English and is the author of many postcards to friends and family!

The bulk of the information in chapter 3 has come from prospectuses produced by the universities themselves, and the many admissions tutors who have helped out with the research also deserve special thanks for tirelessly answering questions with beyond-the-call-of-duty patience.

PREFACE

Over the past few years the number of applicants to the legal profession has increased enormously.

In MPW's work of advising would-be students on their choice of university course, we have gathered together a huge amount of information on Law courses and the legal profession.

With the encouragement of Trotman & Company this information has now been brought together in this guide and supplemented with contributions from Dr James Holland and Julian Webb, lecturers in the Faculty of Law at the University of the West of England.

I am very grateful to the in-house contributors Alastair Boag and Paul Whiteside and also to Joanne Hubert for their research into this topical area of careers advice and I hope that the guide will be of use wherever eager sixth-formers want to know more about getting into Law.

Joe Ruston

INTRODUCTION

☐ WHAT THIS BOOK IS ALL ABOUT

Unless this book has just slipped off the shelf into your hands and fallen open at this very page, you're probably reading it in the hope of picking up some pearls of wisdom on whether or not you should study Law. Well, read on. This guide is intended to answer all those questions you've always wanted to ask and possibly a few more that have never crossed your mind.

Broadly, there are three sections in this book:

- Firstly, there's a brief but down-to-earth description of what legal practitioners actually do and how they fit into the scheme of the legal system, which is explained in Annex B.
- There then follows a selection of ways in which you can become a lawyer and some flow charts to summarise that information.
- The remainder of the book is dedicated to guiding you through the plethora of Law courses on offer and helping you to pick out and secure a place.

Don't be fooled, however, into thinking that *Getting into Law* will do all the work for you so you can put your feet up and watch TV.

This book won't ...
– revise thoroughly and pass your exams on your behalf. Unfortunately this is up to you alone. You can get on to a few university courses with fairly low grades, but those courses might not suit your needs. You'd be better off with higher grades and a consequently wider choice of degrees.

This book won't ...
– talk to your teachers, friends or family, legal practitioners or students or do any other kind of research, like background reading, which you will need to do to decide what type of course is appropriate for *you*. Or, come to that, whether you should even think about studying Law in the first place.

Chapter 1
THE LEGAL PROFESSION

☐ TYPES OF LAWYERS

Most people are familiar with the film and television portrayal of barristers in court robed in wig and gown, confidently destroying a witness with one telling question. Equally, everyone will be familiar with the sight of the Solicitor's office in the High Street where wills are drafted or houses conveyed. But what are the differences between barristers and solicitors (other than the barristers' novel dress sense)? And where do lawyers and attorneys come into it?

The answer is that the legal profession in this country is a split profession. Solicitors are like general practitioners in the medical profession. They have direct and continuing contact with their clients. They will deal with many different aspects of the law, not just those matters which end up in court. Barristers are more like consultants or surgeons. Their main function is to wield the scalpel on behalf of clients referred to them by solicitors and they may only meet their clients on the day of trial. Thus solicitors and barristers should be seen as operating within a loose team, performing different but necessary roles. And to answer the other questions posed in the first paragraph: the term 'lawyer' is simply a collective term for barristers, solicitors, judges, some civil servants, academic lawyers and even law undergraduates; whilst the word 'attorney' refers to American lawyers and now means nothing in English law. We will concentrate here, however, on the distinct types of work undertaken by barristers and solicitors.

Solicitors

For the most part solicitors work in partnerships, known as 'firms'. Some solicitors are in employment, working for large companies as part of their in-house legal departments (eg the trademarks division) but the majority of solicitors are in business in what is termed private practice.These partnerships vary in size a great deal, ranging from two people to hundreds, employing assistant solicitors and trainees as well as the actual partners. The larger the firm the more specialised the individual solicitor's work will be. So a small firm in your local high street may undertake a wide range of activities such as drafting wills, conveying houses, dealing with divorces, sorting out landlord and tenant issues, advising on employment concerns, handling criminal law matters, and sorting out consumer law problems. But no lawyer can hope to be competent in all aspects of the law so many firms may not take on certain work at all.

The larger firms will have specialist departments such as a commercial litigation department, European law department, or one covering employment, shipping law or tax. The list of legal specialisms is extensive. Equally, the depth of expertise required in these areas can sometimes mean that even the larger firms only deal with a narrow range of topics. There is no universal guide as to which firms deal with which matters; though a rule of thumb might be that the smaller firms would be most inclined to take on legal aid work whilst the larger firms will concentrate on litigation and commercial matters.

The main work of solicitors is to act as the first port of call for a client needing help in organising their affairs or as a potential litigant (plaintiff or defendant). If the client needs a will drafting, for instance, the solicitor's work will involve interviewing the client, taking all relevant details and advising on the legal implications of a particular course of action or maybe on the tax strategies to be adopted. The solicitor would then draft the will or other document and, having explained the points to the client, ensure that all the formalities are completed.

If the client is involved in a dispute the solicitor will often try to resolve the matter by writing to the other side. If the dispute continues the solicitor will then have to advise on litigation – the best advice is to avoid litigation at all costs! His or her work will then involve taking statements, collecting evidence and generally preparing the case for trial. In many instances where the amount involved is small and/or where the solicitor is experienced in litigation, the solicitor may then represent the client in court. But here lies a difference between solicitors and barristers: the solicitor can only represent the client in the lower courts, notably the County Court and the Magistrates' court. If the client needs help on a criminal law point the solicitor's work will again entail the gathering of evidence etc, but this time the solicitor may be called upon to visit the police station or prison where the client is in custody in order to take instructions.

The solicitor's work can therefore be extremely varied and has the advantage of direct contact with all different types of people. On the other hand, many solicitors complain that they deal less with legal points and more with matters like interviewing, counselling, paperwork and office management.

Barristers

One of the complaints about the English legal system is that lawyers are like buses: as soon as one appears a whole gang of them arrives. This impression comes from the fact that solicitors may often employ barristers to give specialist advice or to represent the client in court. Thus, instead of hiring only one lawyer, you now have at least two on your hands. The most common question raised here (especially by the client paying two sets of fees) is: why should this be so?

We said earlier that the work of barristers compares with consultants or surgeons; they are specialist advocates. Barristers work as individuals and cannot form partnerships with other lawyers. They do form loose groups called 'chambers' whereby a small number will have their offices in the same building and share the expenses of clerks and common facilities, but these are not firms. Each barrister is responsible for their own caseload.

The solicitor might well want to employ a barrister for two main reasons: first, to gain another opinion on a matter of law from a person who is particularly authoritative in that field of law; secondly, to represent the client in court where the solicitor is not allowed to do so or would prefer a specialist advocate to take on the task. When a solicitor asks for a barrister's view on a legal point this is known as seeking 'counsel's opinion'; where the barrister is asked to undertake litigation work this is known as 'instructing counsel'. If an opinion is sought the barrister will be sent all the relevant paperwork and will sit down and research that area of law before expressing a view as to the merits of the case. If counsel is instructed to act then, generally speaking, the decision to litigate or defend will have been taken (perhaps in the light of an earlier opinion) and the barrister will begin to prepare his or her arguments and, later, actually to argue the case in court. Thus most of the barrister's work will be centred on legal disputes. The barrister acts like the old mediaeval champion: stepping in to fight in the place of the client.

☐ MODERN DISTINCTION

What has been said above is a simplified version of the work of both solicitor and barrister. There are many solicitors who do nothing but litigation work and there are many barristers who concentrate on what is termed 'paper work', providing opinions but rarely if ever appearing in court. Further, the distinctions are being blurred and many people think that before too long we will have a 'fused profession' with no real distinction being made between barristers and solicitors. There is even a move to call everyone an 'attorney'.

Chapter 2
HOW TO BECOME A LAWYER

There are a number of routes into the legal profession as you can see from the diagrams on pages 9-10. The classic route is to take A-levels, read for a law degree (usually called an LLB) and then take a professional course followed by a period of training.

☐ THE STANDARD ROUTE

After A-levels it will normally take three years to gain an LLB, one year to gain the professional qualification and then a further year to become a practising barrister or two years to become a solicitor. Most students will follow this course (a total of five or six years study and training). Nearly all A-levels are acceptable. Legal study is something of a cross between the arts and sciences and so a combination of English, History and Maths would prove a very good grounding in the analytical techniques that will be needed as a Law undergraduate. Contrary to popular belief, taking Law at A-level is not an advantage and some Law Schools will not accept it for admission purposes. It is also quite common for General Studies to be discounted. In all these cases you will need to pay particular heed to each Law School's entrance requirements. You should also note that an A-level language could be an advantage if you apply for a job with one of the big law firms.

☐ DIFFERENT METHODS OF STARTING

A-levels need not be the only entry pathway. Many universities now encourage mature students (who may have missed out on the opportunity to enter Higher Education) to apply for entry on to degree courses, taking into account their work experience and commitment as part of the entry criteria. To facilitate this there are now **Access** courses to be found in Technical Colleges around the country which specifically prepare the mature student for the rigours of higher education in terms of developing learning skills. In many university law faculties, mature students now constitute a third of the intake. The difficulties they face are that they are not as accustomed to study as the A-level entrant, but they possess an advantage in that law is concerned with the everyday practical problems which they may well have faced or more easily appreciate.

Other qualifications may also be acceptable to admissions officers (especially degrees in other disciplines) but there is no common pattern here.

☐ THE DEGREE COURSE

With many Law Schools adopting a modular structure there are now many variations in the design of Law Degrees. Thus you will find courses which concentrate on traditional law subjects, or ones which involve a high percentage of European or comparative law, or joint degrees (eg Law and Politics). In each case you must choose one that suits your interests and possible career path. But if you are going to pursue a career as a barrister or solicitor you will need to ensure that the degree is a Qualifying Degree for Law Society and Bar purposes ie one that is recognised as containing the fundamental principles necessary to move on to professional training. Most LLB courses will be qualifying degrees but you need to check first.

Many courses will allow you to choose optional subjects which will enable some specialism within your course. These options may even extend to non-law subjects such as Forensic Science or Accounts. And in nearly all modern Law degree courses you should expect an emphasis on the acquisition of legal skills, ranging from learning how lawyers think through to advocacy techniques.

☐ EQUIVALENTS TO LAW DEGREES

You can see from the diagram that students from other disciplines can transfer over to legal studies. The most common route is where a graduate in a non-law discipline (eg History) decides to pursue a legal career. He or she will need to take a course which concentrates on the fundamental principles required by the Law Society and Bar (the same subjects which are demanded in a 'Qualifying' law degree. This course is offered by a number of universities and is usually known as the 'Common Professional Examination' or a 'Postgraduate Diploma in Law'. The course is intensive and usually lasts one academic year.

☐ THE PROFESSIONAL QUALIFICATION

As a student you will, at about the start of your second year of undergraduate studies, have had to decide whether to pursue a career as a barrister or solicitor and have begun to make applications to firms or chambers. On graduating you will hope to gain admission to one of the professional courses. To become a solicitor you will need to take one of the Legal Practice Courses offered at various universities. To become a barrister entitled to practise you will need to take the Bar Vocational Course at the Inns of Court School of Law. Both courses last one academic year, are costly, and competition for places is tough. Both courses concentrate on skills-training such as drafting, negotiation and advocacy. If you wish to gain the title of 'barrister' (but not enter practice in the United Kingdom) it is also possible to take a one-year 'non-vocational' course offered by a small number of institutions; though this distinction between the Bar courses is set for change in the near future.

Having passed the Bar's vocational course you may call yourself a barrister. However, you will now need to undertake training as a pupil in chambers. This involves observing a senior barrister (your 'pupil' master) at work for six months (unpaid) followed by a further period of six months where you may appear in court under the loose supervision of your pupil master. You are then on your own, to make as much or as little as your luck and skill allows.

Oddly enough, a student who has passed the Legal Practice course cannot yet be called a solicitor. To gain this title you will need to undertake a 'training contract' in a firm of solicitors which will last two years. During that time you will be instructed in various aspects of legal work, spending time in each department within the firm.

☐ OTHER OPTIONS

Gaining a professional qualification takes time and can cost a lot of money. Equally, many people study law with no intention of becoming a professional lawyer. One of the great advantages of a law degree, however, is that it is recognised as providing one of the best forms of training in terms of analytical ability, attention to detail and logical thought. Law degrees are highly respected in commerce, industry and the civil service. Consequently about forty per cent of all law graduates will not enter the legal profession but will use their degree to pursue other careers. If you choose to study law you should always bear these options in mind.

MAIN ROUTES TO QUALIFYING AS A BARRISTER

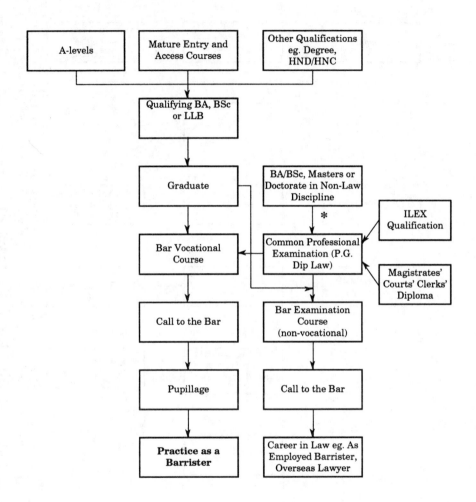

with possibility of exemptions

MAIN ROUTES TO QUALIFYING AS A SOLICITOR

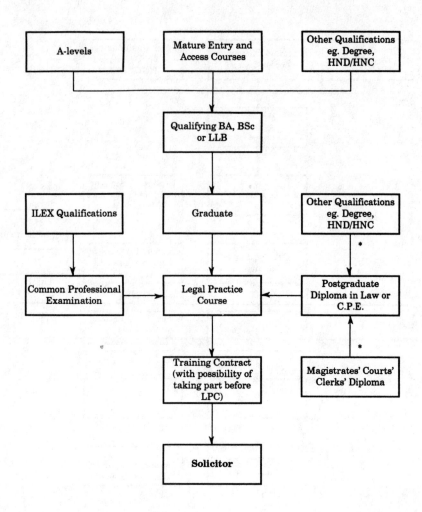

the
MANCHESTER
METROPOLITAN
UNIVERSITY

Meeting your future needs

with over 300 courses in 50 different subject areas...
...one of them will be right for you.

Our mission is to be an accessible institution of higher education meeting the educational and vocational needs of our students and our partners in industry, commerce and the professions.

Being Britain's largest University, we are able to offer an unparalleled choice of undergraduate, postgraduate and professional courses, most of which reflect a primary but not exclusive orientation towards some form of practical education with strong vocational links. We also have an extensive portfolio of research and consultancy activities.

Many of our courses are available in both full-time and part-time modes and a Credit Accumulation & Transfer Scheme (CATS) offers further flexibility and choice.

We have an excellent library, computing and accommodation facilities and our Students' Union offers an extensive range of sporting and recreational activities. We provide a student welfare service which can assist with accommodation, study skills development, personal and financial problems and also provides a careers advice service.

Our main location is in the centre of Manchester, a city renowned for its thriving cultural, social and sporting life. Manchester has been designated Britain's "City of Drama" for 1994 and has some of the most up to date sporting facilities in the country, including a purpose built velodrome. Some of Britain's most beautiful countryside and many other attractions and facilities lie within easy reach of the city.

The former Crewe + Alsager College of Higher Education, located in the Cheshire countryside became a faculty of the University in 1992.

For more information call our 24 hour prospectus hot-line: 061-247 1055, or write to us: The Manchester Metropolitan University, All Saints, Manchester M15 6BH.

Be a little mercenary at university.

This isn't a call for soldiers of fortune. (Money, let's face it, should never be the prime motivation for joining the Forces.)

It's the chance for school leavers, torn between university and the Army, to get the best of both worlds.

All you have to do is meet the challenge of our three-day Officer Selection Board.

Then we'll pay you a total of £25,000 to complete your course at either university or college of higher education, providing you agree to serve as an Officer for at least five years after you graduate.

That means you'll have three times as much to spend as the average student. With the promise of a demanding and exciting job once you've got your Degree.

If you only wish to commit yourself for three years, you can simply apply for a special £1,200 p.a. bursary to supplement any existing grants. But what if you're already halfway through your course?

Providing you have at least one year left to study, you can still benefit from either scheme.

For the full details, just complete the coupon below. And find out how to remain permanently at peace with your bank manager.

For more information about Army Cadetships, please telephone 0345 300111 at any time and quote 0424 (charged at local call rate). Or post this coupon to: Major John Gutteridge, Army Officer Sponsorship, Freepost 4335, Dept. 0424, Bristol BS1 3YX.

Full name_____
                                BLOCK CAPITALS PLEASE
Address_____

_____

_____ Postcode_____

Date of birth_____ Nationality_____

Army Officer

A law degree in itself won't guarantee that you can finish your legal training. And, similarly, being fully qualified won't necessarily mean you'll be able to find work.

Money is an extra hurdle. You'll need a fair amount of it to see you through since an LPC can cost between £3,500 and £6,500 and Bar training anything from £2,500 to £3,800. There are only a limited number of awards, grants and scholarships available.

To get a place on an LPC you need at least a Lower Second Class Honours degree, but as competition increases it doesn't take an Einstein to realise that graduates with Firsts or Upper Second Class degrees stand a better chance. The crunch comes after the LPC when potential lawyers fight for positions as trainee solicitors. This academic year alone will see 6,000 new students hunting down contracts, but only 3,500 of them will be successful (see Annex A).

Those of you pursuing the narrow path to becoming a barrister are also in for a tough time. The selection procedure for the vocational year is a source of much controversy (see Annex A again). This year there were about 2,400 applicants and just 880 places. And after the vocational course, about 25% of those people will be unable to get 'pupillage'.

Chapter 3
CHOOSING YOUR UNIVERSITY LAW COURSE

In the late 1980s, the demand for trainee solicitors actually exceeded the supply. Virtually anyone could pick up articles if they were properly qualified. But, as you no doubt realise now, this Utopia has been turned on its head. And the situation for potential barristers isn't much different – the selection process for the vocational year has changed to allow fewer people in, and the financial hardships experienced during the pupillage year and beyond (despite the availability of more scholarships) deter many. But before, in bleak despair, you start looking up universities offering road resurfacing degrees, think about these points.

(1) The statistics aren't the end of the world. About 50% of law students can end up as practitioners. And who's to say that the 'buds of economic recovery' won't help to change the situation later?

(2) Employers are generally impressed by a law degree, not just because of the high entry requirements, but also because law is a challenging discipline which has, it is hoped, instilled in you a number of relevant skills. It can therefore be your springboard into an ocean of other career possibilities.

And there are areas of law, like Environmental Law and Intellectual Property Law, opening up and other fields are becoming more international. So, once you're past the competitive hurdle, law can present you with a worthwhile and really exciting future.

Assuming then that you still have your heart set on a law degree in some shape or form, there are three basic questions that you must ask yourself, and these make up the core of planning.

☐ PLANNING

Try this quick quiz:
(1) Where do you want to study and in what sort of environment?
(2) What kind of law course are you after?
(3) Will your A-levels be good enough?

How did you score? Only question 3 needs a 'yes' – there are no right answers for the other two. But they are all essential in helping you through the mind-numbing task of selecting what to study and where. From the growing number of institutions offering law courses, it is standard procedure to narrow down the options to, say, 16 or so using the above criteria. This introduction will show you how to do that and will take you through an example.

When you've eliminated 70 or so places (faster than it sounds), look at the relevant pages in this chapter. They are a rough guide on what to expect. But flick through the glossary first so you won't get lost in the jargon. Next, read their prospectuses (both official and alternative) and department brochures (if they exist) for more details, whilst remembering that those publications are designed to sell the course and may be biased! Ideally, after your own research, be it talking to former or current students and legal practitioners, a bit of background reading or visits to the universities themselves, you should end up with eight places to put down on the UCAS form.

The following should throw up some ideas to guide you and help sort out your priorities. When you know what you're looking for turn to the quick reference table to pinpoint all the options that measure up. Then list them on the page provided, first in any order then in order of preference.

The stereotypical image of student life may be one of chaos – an unrevised exam to sit tomorrow and three projects to be typed and submitted yesterday! But it's really in your best interests to be organised and get these selections sorted out early. The notes below should give you a rough idea of what you should be doing at various stages.

During the last term of your lower sixth year

May/June: Do some serious thinking. Get ideas from friends, relatives, teachers, books etc. If possible visit some campuses before you go inter-railing!

June/July/August: Lay your hands on copies of the official and alternative (ie student written) prospectuses and departmental brochures for extra details. They are usually in libraries but it's more reliable to get your own sent to you. Make a shortlist of your courses with the help of this guide.

During your upper sixth year

September: Fill out your application form and give it to your referee for sending off to UCAS – it will be accepted from 1 September onwards.

15 December: This is the deadline for submitting your applications to UCAS. If you wanted to apply to Oxford or Cambridge then you should put your form in before **15 October**. UCAS will still consider late applications, but your chances are limited since some of the places have already gone.

November: The nail-biting starts. Universities hold their interviews and/or open days and start from April to send out their decisions directly to the candidates.

15 May *at the latest*: Or within two weeks of the final decision you receive, you must tell UCAS (assuming you've had some offers) which offer you have accepted firmly and which one is your back-up.

Spring: Fill out yet more forms – this time the grant forms which you can get from your school, college or LEA.

Summer: Sit your exams and await the results! After you get them wait a bit longer and by the end of August you'll know if you've been accepted by a university or college. Don't be too disappointed if you haven't got in. Just get in touch with your school, college or careers office and hang on until September when the left-over places will be filled through 'clearing'. It's up to you to get hold of the published list of these places and contact the universities directly by yourself.

For full details of the UCAS procedure see *How to complete your 1995 UCAS form* (details in the reading list on page 00)

(1) Where in the UK do you want to study and in what sort of environment?

If you're intending to practice law either as a solicitor or barrister or the equivalent, then the question should really be, Where do you want to practice? ...England or Wales? Northern Ireland? Scotland?

Because the legal systems differ over Britain, it seems pretty pointless to study in Aberdeen if you want to practice in Aberystwyth. Although if you do need to move then it is usually possible to transfer the legal skills and knowledge you already have and adapt them to the new place.

(1) How they do it in England and Wales:
Turn to chapter 2 for the run-down on the various routes into the legal profession.

(2) How they do it in Northern Ireland:
Law in N. Ireland is very similar to that in England and Wales, but if you study in Ireland and want to practice over the water then you are obliged to sit an additional exam in Land Law. This should soon be rectified at Queen's University in Belfast which is planning to offer an optional course in English Land Law so students can take all the exemption subjects within their degree. In 1977, the Institute of Professional Legal Studies was set up at the University by the Council of Legal Education. The Council runs a course which can take up to 90 students and provides training for law graduates wishing to become legal practitioners. This vocational course leads to a Certificate in Professional Legal Studies, although its duration depends on whether you train as a barrister or a solicitor. The core subjects you need to start the course are the same as they are in England plus Company Law (or Law of Business Organisations) and Law of Evidence. But if you haven't done these then you have to take a preliminary course for a Certificate in Academic Legal Studies, but only ten students can take advantage of this at QUB. After these certificates you need to find a two year apprenticeship to get your Restricted Practising Certificate so you can work as an assistant solicitor for a few years before you eventually class as a full solicitor, and not before time.

(3) How they do it in Scotland:

Being a lawyer in Scotland (solicitor or advocate) initially involves passing a number of core subjects. The Faculty of Advocates and the Law Society specify eleven common subjects plus two more each. After taking these within your degree there comes a one year postgraduate practical course: a Diploma in Legal Practice. Beyond this, budding solicitors need a two year traineeship to be fully qualified and advocates are required to do yet more practical training and exams on top of that.

Once you've decided which country you'll be in, you can think about choosing a particular region. Some students don't put much stress on this and are fairly geographically mobile, preferring instead to choose the degree course and see where they end up. But university life isn't going to be solely about academic study. Anyone who tells you that, hasn't been to university themselves! It is truly a growing experience – educationally, socially, culturally and besides, three years can really drag if you're not happy outside the lecture theatre! Most can eliminate a couple of areas at least from their list. What follows is an assortment of factors which might have some bearing on where you'd like to study. See which ones you think are relevant to you and try to put them in order of importance.

1) Quality of Teaching. An independent body has been set up by the government to report on the quality of teaching in universities. Only those universities claiming excellence or those for which there are concerns over quality have been assessed. Of these so far, just 16 have been given the classification 'Excellent'. These are listed on page 22.

2) Attractiveness to employers. You will find comments from a number of large firms of solicitors in the Appendix section on page 62-64. These provide some useful advice.

3) Cost of living. Will you be able to reach deeper into your pockets for rent or other fundamentals and entertainment if you are living in a major city or in the South?

4) Accommodation. Is it important to you to live on campus or in halls of residence with other students, or in private housing that you may need to organise yourself and may be a considerable distance from college? Are you a self-catering kind of person? Perhaps you

would prefer someone else cooking for you! Is there any point in moving away from home?

5) Friends and family. Do you want to get away or stay close to them? Whilst you may like the challenge of looking after yourself and the opportunity to be completely independent, there are definitely advantages to living near home, assuming that home is fairly accessible for you.

6) Facilities in and around the university. Apart from the academic resources, which should be all important to prospective students, are you going to be spending much time in, for example, the sports' centre? Are you a theatre-goer or clubber? How about the societies within the student body? Is there one for you to indulge your own hobbies be they common-and-garden or positively bizarre? And if there isn't anything, then would you really be that disappointed?

7) Urban v Rural and Large v Small. Do you yearn for concrete and noise pollution, or would you kill for trees and birdsong? In practice of course, many universities combine the convenience of the city with the atmosphere of the countryside by locating their campus just on the edge of a major town eg University of Nottingham, University of Canterbury etc. But size is a different story. Larger universities may well have better facilities and bigger budgets, but they can overwhelm some students who would be better off in a smaller place where they can at least feel some sense of community.

8) Life after graduation. Yes, there is some, and if you are set on working in a certain area or for a particular institution eg the Home Office, the Law Commission, the Inns of Court and the like, then you may want to study close to that place. If nothing else, you won't have far to move after graduation! Some universities offer the LPC on campus to encourage students to stay on, but this shouldn't rate too highly on your list of priorities.

The question of where to study also encompasses the kind of institution you want to attend. There are many ways of classifying the different types of university, but the only really useful way, without smothering you with pedantic definitions, is to split them into these categories:

a) The Old Universities:

These cover both rural and city sites, but traditionally are set on just one campus and not broken up and splattered over a wide area. Since they are normally well established, they tend to have good libraries and research facilities. Old Universities have a reputation for being resilient to change, but they are gradually introducing modern elements into their degrees. This is more in line with the New Universities, most of whom already offer CATS (Credit Accumulation and Transfer Scheme), modular courses and programmes that make studying abroad infinitely more straightforward, such as Erasmus (see glossary).

b) The New Universities:

These used to be polytechnics or institutes before 1992. Although they may occupy just one site, they are often the product of several colleges and are spread across a number of campuses. They form a separate group because they still hold true to the original polytechnic doctrine of vocational courses and strong ties with industry – typically through placements and work experience. As a student you're likely to have an increased number of contact hours here, but not necessarily a greater workload. And generally the transition from poly to uni happened a bit quickly to cope with the surge of extra students, so there is considerable stress on resources and facilities. Despite their new name, they still suffer discrimination, and many employers honestly believe that a degree from here isn't as good as one from the Old Universities. The New Universities tend to be more flexible about what type of qualifications you need to get in. And they have a better name than the Old Universities for pastoral care. This refers to the relationship between staff and students. The idea being that giving each student a personal tutor – an ear for all academic and social grievances – makes for an easier time at university. The fact that your tutor has a number of other students to listen to, other work, may not be available when you need them and won't insist that you visit them anyway, mean that what is a great idea on paper, doesn't always deliver in practice.

c) The Colleges of Higher Education:

Usually these are specialist institutions and consequently provide excellent facilities in their chosen fields despite their size. They are sometimes affiliated to universities eg Holborn College and the University of Wolverhampton. This form of franchising means the college buys the right to teach the degree, which the university will award, providing that the course meets the standards set by the university.

(2) What kind of Law course do you prefer?

Whilst it's true to say that most universities offer the six current core courses (Law of Contract, Tort, Constitutional and Administrative Law, Criminal Law, Property Law and Equity and Trusts) and the seventh one soon to be made compulsory (Law of the EC), it does not follow that all law courses are the same. Obviously (you're thinking), law can be taken on its own or mixed with a number of other subjects as part of a Joint Honours programme. But no, there's more variety to law degrees than mere course content. You have to decide what teaching/learning approach you like the sound of. There are broadly three types, but only rarely will an institution tell you that it adheres to one kind. Most places are likely to opt for a mixture (sometimes even within individual units) and so this is where your research will come into its own. You must find out what style suits your needs best and which approach is prevalent at specific universities. The categories are:

(1) Black Letter Law
This focuses on the core subjects and doesn't look much beyond statutes and legal reports for its sources of law. It may sound dry, but should provide a thorough grounding in the English legal system. Don't imagine this approach is more fitting for intending practitioners though. There is little statistical evidence to suggest that any one approach is favoured by employers although the Vocational approach may seem more relevant.

(2) Contextual Approach
Some courses like to stick law 'in context', that is to say, Law, its role and its effectiveness are examined in relation to society (past and present), politics and the economy. It doesn't always follow, but courses like this often include elements of Critical Legal Theory. Students are expected to analyse the problems (eg loopholes, contradictions, injustices and so on) within the Law. And this can make for some heated and controversial seminar exchanges! Courses that advertise themselves as producers of liberal, independent thinkers usually mean they take the Contextual approach.

(3) Vocational Approach

This stresses professional training and skills. It includes sandwich degrees with 1 – 12 month work placements and other degrees with units dedicated to 'Lawyers' Skills'. These skills can be reduced to negotiating, interviewing, counselling, drafting, research, analysis, clear expression and the ability to read through vast amounts of material, sift out the legally relevant points and present a logical argument. Ironically, you will be able to pick up most of these skills through other standard law units and extra-curricular activities like mooting (a mock courtroom trial), debating and Law Clinics, where students have the opportunity to help out with a real life case from start to finish.

You now know how you want to be taught, but what about course content? Do you want to study law on its own (a Single Honours degree), with another subject (Joint or Combined degree) or as part of a modular programme alongside a multitude of subject areas? It won't be much help if your only aim is to complete the core subjects since all types of degrees can potentially be qualifying with full exemption from the CPE.

If a Single Honours course sounds interesting, bear in mind that a good range of optional subjects might make it even more inviting. You don't want to be stuck with just a handful of choices from which to fill in your timetable after you've put down the core courses. And options may be law-related or from a completely different discipline. Some places can only offer a limited selection, whilst others provide not just off-the-wall law courses, but the opportunities to take non-law courses from separate faculties and even separate universities! Modular degrees usually have a wide range of subjects and students have an unrestricted choice barring timetable clashes.

Alternatively, if you feel a compulsion to specialise in just one other area, then a Joint degree might be more up your street. Some Joint degrees do not require previous knowledge of the second subject. Others, especially those with a European language often specify that candidates must have an A-level or GCSE level for background knowledge. With Joint degrees, be wary of courses that have seemingly identical titles, for example, Law with German, Law and German and Law and German Law. In the first one, law is the major subject; in the second, you'll probably spend equal time on each and in the third the stress is on German Law rather than German language. Any of them may involve some time abroad.

Studying overseas could be another factor in the race to narrow down your choices. Not all of these courses will make you pack your bags for a full year. And you do not need to be a linguist because you can study overseas in English in, for example, North America, Holland, and the Netherlands.

And some of you will find degrees that include some kind of work placement appealing. Again, these aren't necessarily for a whole year as sandwich courses are not, by definition, four year degrees only.

(3) Will your A-levels be good enough?

Obviously, for the majority of students, their A-level scores will be the decisive means of natural selection. And it's important to be honest about the grades you're heading for. Don't be too pessimistic but, on the other hand, there's no point in kidding yourself about your as yet undiscovered genius. Talk to your teachers for an accurate picture of your predicted grades.

The grades listed in the quick reference table are just for GCE A-levels, but many universities will accept other equivalent qualifications, such as BTEC or GNVQ and Scottish and Irish Highers. Some places specify particular grades but will still take you on if you get the same point score. So, for example, if you are supposed to get ABC (which amounts to 10+8+6 = 24 points), then any combination which produces 24 points (ie BBB or AAD) may be OK.

Not one institution requires law A-level from potential students. Oddly, those of you with a little legal knowledge might even find yourself at a disadvantage. Few courses specify subjects they want you to have studied (with the exception of most European languages Joint degrees which demand you know at least a bit of the relevant language). Conversely, other universities will adamantly reject A-levels like General Studies, or the less academic ones such as Art, whilst traditional qualifications are welcomed everywhere.

If your predicted A-level results effectively prevent you from taking a Law degree, then it's time for a rethink. If you wanted to take a Law degree with a view to entering the profession, then what's wrong with a non-law degree instead?Almost half of new trainee solicitors have a non-law degree. The route might be longer and more expensive, but a graduate with, let's say, an Upper Second Class

21

Honours degree in Philosophy might be more welcome than someone who scraped a Pass in their LLB.

The universities which have so far been categorised as 'excellent' by the University Funding Council are as follows:

Bristol; Cambridge; Durham; Essex; King's College London; Leicester; Liverpool; LSE; Manchester; Northumbria, Newcastle; Nottingham; Oxford, Brookes; University College, London; Sheffield; Warwick; West of England, Bristol.

Please note that not all institutions have been assessed, see p.16 **Quality of Teaching**.

☐ THE QUICK REFERENCE TABLES

These tables are designed to give you some crucial, albeit skeletal, information in a flash. The **first column** defines an area. There are eight in total, namely, London, the South, the Midlands, Wales, the North West, the North East, Scotland and Northern Ireland.

The **second column** gives the name of the institution, and the next column, headed 'type' tells you whether the place is an Old University, a New University or a College of Higher Education.

The **title and duration column** will give the formal name of the degree and the length in years. All of them can be Honours degrees (as opposed to Ordinary degrees) if you work hard enough, so the abbreviation Hons has been left out. But you should note there is a different system in Scotland. To get an Honours degree there, you usually have stay on another year to fit in all the extra courses. The degrees are normally LLBs, that is Bachelor of Law. But there may not be much difference between an LLB and a BA (Bachelor of Arts) or a BSc (Bachelor of Science) in terms of course content. Pondering what letters you want after your name shouldn't really influence your choice of course!

The **qualifying column** simply lets you know if the degree is recognised by the Law Society (of the country in question) as good enough to exempt you from the CPE course after graduation. Warning – you may come across some question marks and this is due to some discrepancies between the Law Society's list and the universities' prospectuses. Unfortunately the printed word can get out of date before you finish the sentence. So, if in doubt, call the university!

If you are keen to see whether you can get some work experience or go overseas to study, then flick across to the **abroad or placement column**. A capital A or P doesn't mean that studying overseas or getting hold of a placement are definite or compulsory. They may be dependent on which optional courses you pick, or on the basis of your academic work. Finally, to check if you can get into the university of your dreams, look at the grades list. Some universities give particular grades, whilst others just demand a certain number of points. Occasionally, no specific entry requirements are given. In these cases the prospectus will usually refer you to their General Entry Requirements section, and the standard criteria is just two A-levels with three other subjects at GCSE level or an epic list of equivalents. Some universities are quite flexible about the grades they ask for, so do some research on their admissions policies. Their published requirements, taken from the UCAS handbook and prospectuses, may just be a guide. And you could still be in with a chance even if you slip a couple of points.

Example

Let's say you want to study in either the Midlands or Wales, you'd like to go to an Old university if possible and a three year qualifying law course is appealing. You don't mind studying law in conjunction with another subject or even spending time abroad or on some kind of work placement, and you are hoping to get BBB (24 points) in your A-levels. Ignoring for the moment the 'E' & '£' marks, you'll end up with the following 20 possibilities:

University	Course title
Birmingham	LLB Law
	LLB Law and Business Studies
	LLB Law and Politics

East Anglia	LLB Law
Essex	LLB Law
Nottingham	BA Law and Politics
Reading	LLB Law
Warwick	BA Law and Sociology
Aberystwyth	LLB Law
	LLB Law, Information and Library Studies
	BSc Law and Economics
	Bsc Law and Poltical Science
	BSc Law, Accountancy and Finance
	BSc Law and Business Studies
Cardiff	LLB Law
	LLB Law and Sociology
	LLB Law and Politics
Swansea	LLB Law
	BA Law with Business
	BA Law with a Language

The Shortlist

For a manageable list of courses, you should have between 10 and 20 options. If you have any more or less then think about your original selection criteria. You don't want to swamp yourself with too many to sift through, but on the other hand too few might reduce your chances of getting an offer.

When you've got this far, scribble down the possible courses below. First put them in any order, then after you've read the relevant pages and done your own research, put them down in order of preference alongside.

In any order:			*In order of preference:*		
Uni.	Course	Req's	Uni.	Course	Req's
1			1		
2			2		
3			3		
4			4		
5			5		
6			6		
7			7		
8			8		
9			9		
10			10		
11			11		
12			12		
13			13		
14			14		
15			15		
16			16		
17			17		
18			18		
19			19		
20			20		

Quick Reference Tables

LONDON AREA

University	type	title and duration (years)		qualifying	abroad or place't	grade
Brunel	old	LLB Law	3/4	yes	P	24
		LLB Business & Financial Law	3/4	yes	P	24
		BSc Government with Law	3/4	yes	P	24
		BSc Economics with Law	3/4	yes	P	24
		BSc Management with Law	3/4	yes	P	24
City	old	LLB Business Law	3	yes		BBB
East London	new	LLB/BA Law	3	yes		14-16
		BA Law & Accounting	3	yes		"
		BA Social Science	3	yes		"
		BA Combined Studies	3	yes		"
Greenwich	new	LLB/BA Law	3	yes		20
Kingston	new	LLB Law	3	yes		BCC
		LLB Law with Euro/ International Legal Systems	4	?		ACCC
		BA Accounting & Law	3	yes		"
London: KCL	old	LLB Law	3	yes		AAB
		LLB English & French Law	4	yes	A (2 yrs)	ABB
		LLB Law with German Law	4	yes	A	"
London: LSE	old	LLB Law	3	yes		BBB
		LLB Law with French/German	4	yes	A	"
		BA Law & Anthropology	3	yes		"
		BSc Law & Government	3	yes		"
London: QMWC	old	LLB Law	3	yes		BBB
		LLB English & Euro Law	4	yes	A	"
		BA Law & Economics	3	yes		BBC
		BA Law & Politics	3	yes		"
		LLB Law with German	4	?	A	BBB
		BA Law & German	4	no	A	18
London: SOAS	old	LLB Law	3	yes		BBC
		BA Joint Law	3	yes		"
London: UCL	old	LLB Law/with Adv Studs	3/4	yes		A/BBB
		LLB Law with French Law	4	yes	A	"
		LLB Law with German Law	4	yes	A	"
		LLB Law with Italian Law	4	yes	A	"
		LLB Law & History	3	yes		"

University	type	title and duration (years)		qualifying	abroad or place't	grade
Guildhall	new	LLB Business Law	3	yes		18-20
		LLB Law	3	yes		"
		BA Legal Studies	3	yes		"
		BA Modular	3	no		DD-BC
Middlesex	new	LLB Law	3	yes		18
		BA/BSc Modular	3	yes		18
North London	new	LLB Law	3	yes		CCC-BB
		BA Law in Bus & Bus Econ	3	no		"
		BA Law in Bus & Employ't Stud	3	no		"
South Bank	new	LLB Law	3	yes		B/CCC
Thames Valley	new	LLB Law	3	yes		18
		LLB Law with Fr Law & Lang	4	yes	A	B/CCC
		LLB Law with Germ Law & Lang	4	yes	A	"
		LLB Law with Span Law & Lang	4	yes	A	"
		BA Accounting & Law	3	yes		"
		BA European Law	3	yes	A (2 sem.)	"
		BA Criminal Justice	3	yes		18
Westminster	new	LLB Law	3	yes		BCC
		LLB European Legal Studies	4	yes	A	"
		BA Social & Policy Science	3	no		"
		BA Law & Language	3	yes		"

THE SOUTH

University	type	title and duration (years)		qualifying	abroad or place't	grade
Bournemouth	new	LLB Business Law	44	yes	P	20
		BA Tax & Revenue Law	3	no		20
Bristol	old	LLB Law	3	yes		26
		LLB Law & French	4	yes	A	26
		LLB Law & German	4	yes	A	26
		LLB European Legal Studies	4	yes	A	26
Bristol UWE	new	LLB Law	3	yes		20
		LLB European Law & Language	4	yes	A	22
Exeter	old	LLB Law	3	yes		26
		LLB European Law	4	yes	A	26
		BA Law & Society	4	yes		not given
		BSc Chemistry & Law	4	yes		"

THE SOUTH CONT...

University	type	title and duration (years)		qualifying	abroad or place't	grade
Kent	old	LLB Law	3	yes		24-26
		LLB English & French Law	4	yes	A	"
		LLB English & German Law	4	yes	A	"
		LLB English & Spanish Law	4	yes	A	"
		LLB English & Italian Law	4	yes	A	"
		LLB European Legal Studs	4	yes	A	"
		BA Combined Studies	3	yes		"
Plymouth	new	LLB Law (Comb'd Studs)	3	yes		BCC
		LLB with Another	3	no		"
Southampton	old	LLB Law	3	yes		ABB
		BSc Accounting & Law	3	yes		not given
		BSc Politics & Law	3	yes		"
		BA Business & Law	3	?		10
		BA Accounting & Law	3	no		10
Southampton Institute	coll	LLB Law	3	yes		16
Surrey	old	BSc French & Law	4	yes	P (abroad)	BBC
		BSc German & Law	4	yes	"	BCC
		BSc Russian & Law	4	yes	"	BBC
Sussex	old	LLB Law	3	yes		BBB
		LLB European Commercial Law	4	yes	A	"
		BA Law with American Studies	4	yes	A	"
		BA Law & Economics	3	yes		"
		BA Law with History	3	yes		"
		LLB/BA Law with French/German/ Italian/ Spanish or Russian	4	yes	P (abroad)	

THE MIDLANDS

University	type	title and duration (years)		qualifying	abroad or place't	grade
Anglia Poly Uni	new	LLB Law	3	yes		18
		BA Combined	3/4	yes		18
Birmingham	old	LLB Law	3	yes		24-30
		LLB Law with French	4	yes	A	24-30
		LLB Law & Business Studies	3	yes		24-30
		LLB Law & Politics	3	yes		24-30
		LLB Law & European Law	4	yes	A	24-30

University	type	title and duration (years)		qualifying	abroad or place't	grade
Bucking-ham	old	LLB Law (Language Options)	2	yes	A	18
		LLB European Studies	2	yes		18
		LLB Law, Biology & the Enviro	2	yes		18
		LLB Politics & Law & Economics	2	yes	18	
Cambridge	old	BA Law Tripos	3	yes		AAA-B
Central England	new	LLB Law	3	yes		18
		BA Government	3	no		14
Coventry	new	LLB Law	3	yes		20
		LLB European Business Law	4	yes		20
		LLB Business Law	3	yes		18
		LLB Criminal Justice	3	yes		20
		BA Law & Intern'l Studies	3	no		20
De Montfort	new	LLB Law	3	yes	P	20
		LLB Law with French	4	yes	A	20
		LLB Law with German	4	yes	A	20
		BA/BSc Combined Studies	3	yes		20
Derby	new	LLB Law	3	yes		not given
		BA/BSc Modular	3	no		10
East Anglia	old	LLB Law	3	yes		24
		LLB Law with Ger/Fr Lang & Law	4	yes	A	24
		LLB Law with Europ'n Legal Sys	4	yes	A	24
		LLB Law with American Studies	4	?	A	24
Essex	old	LLB Law	3	yes		24
		LLB English & European Law	4	yes	A	24
		LLB English & French Law	4	yes	A	24
Hertfordshire	new	LLB Law	3	yes		BCC
		BSc Combined Studies	3	yes		"
		BA Social Science	3	yes		"
Leicester	old	LLB Law	3	yes		ABB
		LLB Law (EC Route)	4	yes	A	"
		LLB Law with French	4	yes	A	"
		BA Economics & Law	3	?		BBB
Luton	coll	LLB Law	3	yes		14
Nene	coll	BA Combined Studies	3	yes		not given
		BA Law	3	?		18

University	type	title and duration (years)		qualifying	abroad or place't	grade
Nottingham	old	LLB/BA Law	3	yes		ABB
		BA Law & Politics	3	yes		BBB
		BA Law with American Law & Pol	4	yes	A	"
		BA Law with Euro Law & Politics	4	yes	A	"
		BA Law with American/Euro Law	4	yes	A	"
Nottingham Trent	new	LLB Law	3	yes		20-26
		LLB Law (sandwich)	4	yes		20-26
		LLB European with Fr/Ger	4	?	A	20-26
		BA Public Administration	3	no		not given
		BA Government & Public Policy	3	no		not given
Oxford	old	BA Jurisprudence	3	yes		AAB
		BA Law with Fr/Ger or Euro Law	4	yes	A	"
Oxford Brookes	new	LLB Law	3	yes		BBB-C
		BA Law & Another	3	yes		"
		BA Modular	3	no		BBC
Reading	old	LLB Law	3	yes		ABC
		LLB Law with French Law	4	yes	A	ABB
		LLB Law with Euro Legal Studies	4	yes	A	ABC
Warwick	old	LLB Law	3/4	yes		ABB
		LLB European Law	4	yes	A	AAB
		BA Law and Sociology	4	yes		BBB
Wolverhampton	new	LLB Law	3	yes		22
		LLB Law with Language	4	yes	A	22
		BA Law (modular)	3	yes		16

WALES

University	type	title and duration (years)		qualifying	abroad or place't	grade
Aberyswyth	old	LLB/BA Law	3	yes		24
		LLB Law & European Language	4	yes	A	24
		LLB Law, Info & Library Studies	3	?		24
		BSc Law & Economics	3	yes		24
		BSc Law & Political Science	3	yes		24
		BSc Law, Accounting & Finance	3	yes		24
		BSc Law & Business Studies	3	yes		24
Cardiff	old	LLB Law	3	yes		BBB
		LLB Law & Fr/Ger/Ital/Span/Jap	4	yes	A	A/BBB

WALES CONT...

University	type	title and duration (years)		qualifying	abroad or place't	grade
		LLB Law & Sociology	3	yes		22-26
		LLB Law & Politics	3	yes		22-26
Glamorgan	new	LLB Law	3	yes		20
Gwent	coll	BSc Accounting & Legal Studies	3	no		not given
		BSc Business & Legal Studies	3	no		not given
Swansea	old	LLB Law	3	?		BBB
		BA Law with Business	3	?		BBB
		BA Law with Fr/ Germ/ Italian/ Spanish/ Russian or Welsh	3	?		BBC
Swansea Insti	coll	LLB Law	3	yes		BC

THE NORTH WEST

University	type	title and duration (years)		qualifying	abroad or place't	grade
Central Lanc	new	LLB Law	3	yes		BCC
		LLB Law & French	4	yes	A	CCC
		LLB Law & German	4	yes	A	"
		BA/BSc Law (Combined)	3	yes		"
Keele	old	BA Law & Another	3	yes		BBB
Lancaster	old	LLB Law	3	yes	A	24
		LLB European Legal Studies	4	yes	A	24
Liverpool	old	LLB Law	3	yes		ABB
		LLB Law & French	4	yes	A	"
		LLB Law & German	4	yes	A	"
Liverpool John Moore's	new	LLB/BA Law	3	yes		BCC
		BA Combined Studies	3	no		"
Manchester	old	LLB Law	3	yes		ABB
		LLB English & French Law	4	yes	A	"
		BA Accounting & Law	4	yes	P (6 weeks)	BBB
Manch'er Metro.	new	LLB Law	3	yes		18
		LLB Law with French	4	yes	P (abroad)	18
Staffordshire	new	LLB/BA Law	3	yes	A	BCC
		BA Legal Studies	3	no		CCC
		BA Joint/ Combined Law	3	yes		"
		BA Joint/ Combined Legal Stud's	3	no		"

THE NORTH EAST

University	type	title and duration (years)		qualifying	abroad or place't	grade
Durham	old	LLB Law	3	yes		26
		LLB European Legal Studies	4	yes	A	26
		BA Law & Economics	4	yes		26
		BA Law & Politics	4	yes		26
		BA Law & Sociology	4	yes		26
Huddersfield	new	LLB Law	3	yes		18
		LLB Business Law	3	yes		18
Hull	old	LLB Law	3	yes	A	BBB
		BA Gender Studies with Law	3	no		BCC
		BA Law & Sociology	3	no		"
		BA Law with Philosophy	3	no		"
		BA Law & Politics	3	n		"
Humberside	new	BA Law & Business	3	yes	AP	16
Leeds	old	LLB Law	3	yes		ABB
		LLB Law with a European Law	3	yes	A	"
		LLB Law & Chinese Studs	4	yes	A	BBB
		LLB Law & Japanese Studies	4	yes	A	"
		LLB Law & French Studies	4	yes	A	ABB
Leeds Metro.	new	LLB Law (Modular)	3	yes		CCC
Newcastle	old	LLB Law	3	yes		ABB
		BA Accounting & Law	3	yes		BBB
Northumbria	new	LLB Law	3/4	yes		BBB
				(+LPC)		
		LLB French & English Law	4	yes		"
Sheffield	old	LLB/BA Law	3	yes	A	ABB
		BA Law & Criminology	3	yes		"
		BA Law with Fr/Ger or Spanish	4	yes	A	"
Sheffield Hallam	new	LLB/BA Law	3/4	yes	AP	20
		BA International Fin'l Studies	4	no	A	20
Teesside	new	LLB Law	3	yes		CCC
		BA Accounting/ Law	3	no		"

SCOTLAND

University	type	title and duration (years)		qualifying	abroad or place't	grade
Aberdeen	old	LLB Law (Lang options)	3/4	yes	A	22
		LLB Law & French Law/ Lang	4/5	yes	A	22
		LLB Law & Germ Law / Lang	4/5	yes	A	22
		LLB Law & Belgian Law	4/5	yes	A	22
		LLB Law & European Legal Studies	4/5	yes	A	22
		LLB Law with Economics	3/4	yes		22

SCOTLAND CONT...

University	type	title and duration (years)		qualifying	abroad or place't	grade
Dundee	old	LLB Law	3/4	yes (+Eng)		24
		LLB Law/Arts/Soc Sci Subj	3/4	?		24
Dundee Institute	coll	BA European Business Law	3/4	?		10
		BA Legal Studies	3/4	?		10
Edinburgh	old	LLB Law	3/4	yes		26
		BA Combined	3/4	yes		26
Glasgow	old	LLB Law		yes		26
		LLB Law with European Lang	3/4	yes		26
Glas. Caledon'n	new	BA Law with Admin Studies	3/4	no		CCE
Napier	new	BA Legal Studies	3/4	no		CCC
Robert Gordon	new	BA Legal & Admin Studies	3/4	no		10
Stirling	old	BA Business Law (Ord)	3	no		B/ CBC
Strathclyde	old	LLB Law	3/4	yes		24
		LLB European Law	3/4	yes	A	24
		BSc Computer Sci with Law	3/4	no		CCC

NORTHERN IRELAND

University	type	title and duration (years)		qualifying	abroad or place't	grade
Belfast	old	LLB Law	3	yes (+Eng)		ABB
		LLB Law & Accounting	4	yes		"
		LLB Law with French	4	yes	A	"
		LLB Law with German	4	yes	A	"
		LLB Law with Hispanic Studies	4	yes	A	"
		LLB Law with Italian	4	yes	A	"
Ulster	old	BA Government & Law	3	yes		BBC
		BA Law & Economics	3	yes		"

Chapter 4
COMPLETING YOUR UCAS FORM

General advice on filling in your UCAS form is given in another guide in this series, *How to Complete Your UCAS Form*, co-written by Dr Tony Higgins, Joint Chief Executive of UCAS. (See Reading List).

The following advice is directed at helping you complete Section 10, your personal statement. This is your opportunity to explain to the university admissions staff why you want to study Law.

☐ FILLING IN YOUR PERSONAL SECTION

The personal section of the UCAS form is the only chance you get to recommend yourself as a serious candidate worthy of a place, or at least, worthy of an interview. It is therefore vital that you think very carefully indeed about how to complete it so that it shows you in the best possible light. You must sell yourself to the department of law and make it hard for them not to take you.

Obviously, there are as many ways of completing your Section 10 as there are candidates. There are no rules as such, but there are recommendations that can be made.

Universities are academic institutions and thus you must present yourself as a strong academic bet. The first thing that the admissions tutor reading your form wants to know is the strength of your commitment to academic study. Say clearly why you wish to study law. Money, status, family traditions, the sound of your own voice and legal paraphernalia are not good reasons. Give details and examples of what precisely it is about the law that interests you, referring to recent cases, controversies and debates. Explain what you hope to get out of three years of legal academic study. Refer to cases that you have followed in detail. Tell the admissions tutor what related material you have recently read and explain why you appreciated it. What recent judgments have you admired recently and why? What legal controversies have excited you? Which particular branch of the law interests you most and – again – why? Which lawyers, either living or dead, have inspired you and for what reason?

Work experience is useful as it demonstrates a commitment to the subject outside the classroom. If you have had relevant work experience talk about it on your form. Explain concisely what your job entailed.

Future plans can also be included on your form, if you have any. Be precise. Again this will demonstrate a breadth of interest in the subject.

At least half of your section 10 should deal with material directly related to your chosen course. Thereafter, use the rest of the page – you must use it all – to tell the admissions tutor what makes you who you are. What travel have you undertaken? What do you read? What sporting acheivements do you have? What music do you like or play? In all these things give details. This is weak:

Last year I went to France. I like reading and listening to music and sometimes I play football at weekends.

A stronger version could read:

Last year I went to Paris and visited all the Impressionist galleries there. I relax by reading American short stories – Andre Dubus, Raymond Carver amongst others. My musical taste is largely focused on opera (I have seen 14 productions of `The Magic Flute') and I would like to continue playing the `cello in an orchestra at university. I would also enjoy the chance to play in a football team to keep myself fit.

Make them want to teach you; make them want to meet you.

Chapter 5
SUCCEEDING IN YOUR INTERVIEW

Outside Oxford and Cambridge and for certain courses such as medicine, formal interviews are rarely part of the admissions process. They are expensive and time-consuming for both the university and the applicants. Nevertheless, our research shows that sixth-formers do worry about interviews and we wanted to include advice on them in this guide.

Also, it's worth bearing in mind that if you shine in your interview and impress the admissions staff no end, then they may drop their grades slightly and make you a lower offer in the hope that you will join them, even if you slip a couple of points in your exams.

Every interview is a character-building experience and need not be as daunting as most candidates fear. There are a number of practical steps that can be taken to reduce the anxiety that inevitably occurs when strangers ask you demanding questions.

While the number of people conducting the interview and the length of time it takes can vary, all interviews are designed to enable those asking the questions to find out as much about the candidate as they can. It is important, therefore, to engage actively with the process (good eye-contact and confident body language help here) and view it as a chance to put yourself across rather than as an obstacle course designed to catch you out.

Interviewers are more interested in what you know than what you do not. If you are asked a question to which you do not know the answer, say so. To waffle (or worse, to lie) simply wastes time and lets you down. The interviewers will be considering the quality of thought that goes into your answers; they will not expect you to know everything already. Pauses while you think are completely acceptable; do not be afraid to take your time.

It is important to remember that there is a strong chance that amongst the people interviewing you will be those who will actually tutor you during your time at university. Enthusiasm for, and a strong commitment to your subject and, above all, a willingness to learn are therefore extremely important attitudes to convey. The people you meet at interview not only have to judge your academic calibre but also have to evaluate whether they would enjoy teaching you for the next three or four years.

An ability to think on your feet is vital. Pre-learned answers never work; they appear glib and superficial and no matter how apparently spontaneously they are delivered, they are always detectable. Putting forward an answer step by step, using examples and factual knowledge to reinforce your points will impress interviewers far more, even if you are uncertain of what you say. Obviously, this is especially true for candidates wishing to read literary subjects like law, but the general principle applies across the board. That said, it is also sensible to admit defeat if your argument is demolished. Knowing you are beaten is a more intelligent thing to do than mindlessly clinging to the wreckage of a specious case.

It is possible to steer the interview yourself to some extent. If, for example, you are asked about something about which you know nothing, confidently replacing that question with another related one yourself shows enthusiasm. (This requires a bit of care however, since you don't want to appear arrogant coming to an interview and supplying your own questions!) It is important that time is not wasted in silences that are as embarrassing for the interviewer as for the candidate.

Essential preparation includes revision of the personal section of your UCAS form and it is therefore not wise to include anything on your form about which you are unprepared to speak. This document may well form the basis of preliminary questions.

Questions may well be asked on your extra-curricular activities. Most often, this is a tactic designed to put you at your ease and therefore your answers should be thorough and enthusiastic but you should avoid spending too long over them.

At the end of the interview, those conducting it may well ask if there is anything you would like to ask them. If there is nothing, then say that your interview has covered all that you had thought of. It is sensible though, to have one or two questions of a serious kind – to do with the course, the tuition and so on – up your sleeve. It is not wise, obviously, to ask them anything that you could and should have found out from the prospectus. It is also permissible and even desirable to ask a question based on the conversations that have made up the interview. This marks you out as someone who listens, is curious and who is willing to learn.

Above all, make them remember you when they go through a list of twenty or more candidates at the end of the day.

☐ PREPARATION FOR A LAW INTERVIEW

We are assuming that you will be taking a Single Honours Law degree, but if you have chosen a Joint or Combined Honours course, then obviously you will have to prepare yourself for questions on those subjects as well. This is particularly important if you have opted to study a language which requires a stint of study abroad.

Whether you have studied for a law A-level or not, the interview is a chance for you to demonstrate knowledge of, commitment to and enthusiasm for the theories and practice of the law. The only way to do this is to be extremely well-informed. Interviewers will be looking for a breadth of engagement with the subject that extends well beyond school or college and A-level courses. They will want to know your reasons for wishing to study law and, possibly above all, they will be looking to see whether you have a mind capable of developing logical arguments and the ability to articulate such arguments powerfully and coherently. Given that much of the practice of law in this country rests on an adversarial system, it would be foolish to be unprepared for an adversarial interview.

Reasons for wishing to study law vary. A passion for courtroom drama, The Bill or LA Law is not enough. You need to think about the everyday practice of the law in this country and it is extremely useful to spend time talking with lawyers of all kinds and learning from them what is involved.

It is obviously also important to be aware of the many types of law that lawyers practice – criminal, contract, family, taxation to name a few – and to be clear about the differences between them. The essential differences between barristers and solicitors (itself a controversial issue) must also be clear in your mind. It is also appropriate to know in detail the various routes into the law after university, and what you can expect in terms of promotion, salary, workload and so on. If you are a woman, these issues become all the relevant as the law remains very much a male-dominated profession.

☐ THE MEDIA

As a serious A-level candidate you will already be reading a daily newspaper. For the purposes of preparing for a law degree, this is vital. *The Independent*, *The Times* and *The Guardian* all have law sections during the week (on Tuesdays, Thursdays and Fridays respectively). Following detailed law reports in the press will give you further insight into the ways in which the law is practised.

Reading these pages not only helps keep you abreast of current events but also gives you the opportunity to see how the language of the law is used in practice and, if you have been studying the subject at A-level, how what you have learnt in the classroom applies to the real world.

Understanding the legal implications of current affairs is essential and regular listening to the radio and watching television are vital. Much of the news has legal implications and these subjects are consistently discussed in the broadcast media. TV's 'Question Time', 'Newsnight' and certain 'Panorama' style documentaries and radio's 'The Today Programme', 'The World This Weekend' and 'Today in Parliament' are all examples of potentially very useful programmes to help you build up a thorough knowledge of current events.

Knowledge of the structure of the legal and judicial systems is vital. You should know who the Lord Chief Justice is, who the Director of Public Prosecutions is and what he or she does. You should be aware of recent controversial legal decisions, who took them and what their consequences are or could be. Who is the Home Secretary and why is he or she important? What do you think should be happening in the prison system at the moment? What reforms would you like to see implemented in the running of the police force? Should the police be armed in this country? Should the right to silence be upheld?

☐ INTERVIEW QUESTIONS

Some of these areas are covered in the Annexes at the end of this guide and there is also a list of books for further reading.

Interviewers will ask questions with a view to being in a position to form an opinion about the quality of your thought and your ability to argue a particular case. The more informed you are, the better able you will be to stick to your guns and to have precise legal and judicial references with which to back up your arguments. You may be presented with a real or supposed set of circumstances and then be asked to comment on the legal implications of them. The questions fired at you could be general – Is euthanasia wrong? What is the purpose of prison? – or extremely particular – What is the difference between burglary and theft? Should the voice of Gerry Adams be heard on mainland TV and radio?

Recent events are very likely to form a large part of the interview. Ethical issues, political issues, police issues, prison reform issues – all of these are possible as the basis for questions at interview and you should have thought about the vast majority of them and be able to expound the main arguments on either side of whatever particular case you are presented with. An ability to see the opposite point of view while maintaining your own will mark you out as strong law degree material.

Finally, don't forget that interview skills are greatly improved by practice. Chat through the issues we have discussed with your friends and then arrange for a teacher or family friend to give you one or more mock interviews. You will find that recording the interview on video for later analysis is very useful.

In this section we shall consider a number of current issues concerning the English Legal System. These should give you a brief flavour of what studying law is about, and also provide you with some ammunition for discussion (if necessary) if you are called for interview by a university law school.

We have chosen three topics for consideration, two relating to the criminal, and one to the civil process. There are no absolute answers to the questions posed. They are designed to stimulate your own thoughts and lead to some wider reading.

☐ MISCARRIAGES OF CRIMINAL JUSTICE

The term 'miscarriage of justice' is widely used, but seldom defined. The Royal Commission on Criminal Justice (1993) – the Runciman Commission – recognised that the term could incorporate the acquittal of the guilty as well as the conviction of the innocent, but it is miscarriages in the latter sense that have been the greatest concern in recent years. Indeed, over the past four or five years it has, at times, been hardly possible to open a newspaper without being presented with revelations of yet another miscarriage of justice. What has been happening to the English criminal justice system?

In looking at the problems I would suggest the first and fundamental question is – what leads to wrongful conviction? There are at least four prime causes to consider.

Mistakes of fact

These are, in a sense, the least controversial aspect of the problem. Wrongful convictions may arise where no one is truly at fault. This is because the conviction will appear correct on the evidence available at the time, but that evidence later proves to be incomplete or inaccurate. For example, where evidence supporting an accused's alibi only comes to light after the trial; or where flaws in the forensic evidence against an accused were not identifiable given the state of scientific knowledge at the time of trial.

There are some safeguards in the present system which try to identify and prevent these errors, but there is obviously a limited capacity in any system of justice to stop such mistakes happening. Whether present safeguards are adequate is one of points of debate at present. Critics of the English system, which involves a process of review by the Court of Appeal, argue that it is inadequate for the job, being too slow, and some would say overly reluctant to admit that judge and jury initially got it wrong. The **Birmingham Six**, the alleged IRA activists who had been wrongly convicted of bombing two Birmingham pubs in 1974, had their case reviewed three times by the Court of Appeal before their convictions were finally quashed in 1991.

Procedural Inequality

The defence lawyer Michael Mansfield QC is one who has strongly argued that one of the problems of the English system is that the defence are placed at a disadvantage from the outset.

He argues, for example, that the defence lack the physical and financial resources of the state, and may not be able to pursue the defence as rigorously as they would like. Forensic evidence of the crime provides a key case in point. It is gathered and tested by Home Office forensic scientists. Although the results are made available to the defence, there is a general shortage of independent forensic services to enable the defence to carry out its own assessment and testing of the evidence. Does this fit in with our sense of justice and due process?

Procedural or Tactical Error

The defence itself may make significant mistakes which undermine the position of their client.This may involve a tactical error, eg, allowing a weak and unconvincing accused to testify in his or her own defence, when it would have been better to rely on the right of silence; or a procedural failure – either at the trial or earlier.

In the **Cardiff Three** case, for example, one of the accused, a young man with serious learning difficulties, was questioned in a manner which the Court of Appeal later condemned as 'oppressive'. At the interview he was represented by a solicitor, who did not intervene at all on his client's behalf. The interview resulted in a confession which in turn led to the conviction of the Three for the murder of a prostitute. Not surprisingly, when the convictions were quashed by the Court of Appeal [R v Paris, Millar & Abdullahi (1992)], the judges were highly critical ofthe solicitor's failure to protect his client's interests.

This kind of thing has obviously heightened concerns about the quality of representation and advice that defendants in criminal trials receive. How do we improve access to advice and resources for the accused? Should we even try, or is inequality an inevitable feature of the criminal justice system?

Procedural Impropriety

One of the greatest causes of concern is the extent to which misconviction is the result of deliberate or negligent behaviour by participants in the criminal justice system. Cases have disclosed impropriety by the police; by expert witnesses; by prosecution counsel and by the judge.

(a) Police malpractice has been a substantial cause of many of the major miscarriages of justice. To be sure, cases such as the **Birmingham Six** and **Guildford Four** pre-dated the reforms to the procedural rules governing the police, introduced in the Police and Criminal Evidence Act 1984 (PACE), but this is not an adequate explanation. A number of the more recent miscarriages have involved breaches of PACE. Most of these cases involve breaches of the rules governing the detention and questioning of suspects. Thus, the conviction, in 1988, of **Jacqueline Fletcher**, a 28 year old woman with a mental age of 10, who confessed to murdering her baby, was overturned in 1992 because of flagrant abuse of questioning procedures. The convictions of the **Darvell Brothers** in 1986 were also quashed for police impropriety. 'Confessions' had been rewritten by the police; identification evidence had been fabricated, and fingerprints which would have helped exonerate the accused were not fully investigated, and destroyed before the trial.

These examples suggest that some fairly fundamental problems still remain in policing practice. What is it about existing methods and procedures that encourage the police, at least in some cases, to find a suspect and that make sure that the evidence fits? Is the problem purely one of a few rogue officers, or is it more fundamental than that? How do we stop these things happening?

(b) Malpractice by the prosecution has been unearthed in a number of instances. **Stefan Kisko's** conviction for the murder of a young girl was quashed in 1992, after he had spent 17 years in prison. It was discovered that evidence showing that fertile semen had been found on the girl's body was not disclosed at the trial. Kisko was infertile. Evidence was also suppressed in the case of the **Darvell Brothers** (above).

(c) Impropriety by the judge, in the form of a prosecution bias, has also been an occasional concern. Cases have arisen where judges have summed-up a case to the jury in a less than impartial manner (Mr Justice Bridge's summing-up in the trial of the **Birmingham Six** was a prime example of this). But in other situations the problem is much less overt – where, for example, the judge has taken an uncritical approach to allegations of police misconduct, or to dubious forensic evidence (again the IRA cases of the **Guildford Four**, **Birmingham Six**, **Maguire Seven** and **Judith Ward** offer examples of these problems).

Perhaps in some ways these latter instances are the most disturbing of all. In English law the criminal trial is supposed to proceed on an assumption that an accused is innocent until proven guilty. If the lawyers and judges are themselves guilty of, at worst, falsely, at best, recklessly, constructing the guilt of the accused, what conclusions should we draw about the reliability of the criminal trial process?

I have not attempted to give you answers to all the questions that these miscarriages of justice surely raise. The Runciman Commission was set up in 1991 to propose its own solutions, but these are themselves the subject of hot debate in both the academic and the national press.

☐ THE FUTURE OF TRIAL BY JURY

When non-lawyers conjure-up an image of a trial, an integral element will almost certainly be the jury. The principle of trial by jury is rooted in the medieval origins of English law, and it remains a powerful part of the ideology of law.

In theory, everyone retains the right to 'trial by one's peers', and jury trial is widely represented as a safeguard against oppressive government or the conviction-minded judge. But what is the reality behind this rhetoric?

The Process of Jury Trial

Any citizen who is over 18 and under 65, who is not disqualified by virtue of some specific rule, may be required to do jury service. Juries are selected randomly on a local basis from the electoral register. If you are selected, you will be expected to attend your local Crown Court centre with other potential jurors. Each jury must consist of 12 persons. More jurors will be called for service than will actually be 'empanelled' on a specific jury.

Once empanelled, it is the task of the jury to be the triers of fact. This means it is the jury's decision whether or not a person is innocent or guilty on the evidence presented in court. The jury is advised as to the law by a professionally qualified judge, but the decision on the facts is theirs alone. The jury's decision, or 'verdict' is given at the end of the trial, in open court. It must normally be a unanimous one, though in exceptional circumstances, the judge may accept a majority verdict. Where the result is a guilty verdict, then the sentence is determined by the judge, not the jury.

The Scope of Trial by Jury

The first point to be aware of is that the right to trial by jury has diminished steadily and substantially since the nineteenth century. Then juries sat on all but the most minor civil and criminal trials. The right to a jury in civil proceedings was the first to be eroded, until today there are very few civil matters where the option to trial by jury really exists. The decline of jury trial in criminal cases has been rather less dramatic, but far more contentious.

The basic principle in criminal cases is that a defendant will be tried by jury in relation to any offence that is triable in the Crown Court. This court has jurisdiction over a wide range of offences, including the most serious crimes, such as murder, manslaughter, rape and arson, but also many lesser offences against the person or property. Even so, on average, less than 10% of all criminal trials are heard before the Crown Court, with the remainder being dealt with by Justices of the Peace in the Magistrates' Courts. Over the years, there has been a gradual process of reclassifying offences, so that they come within the jurisdiction of the Magistrates' Courts only. Such changes were made by legislation in 1977 and again in 1988.

The Runciman Commission, in one of its most controversial conclusions, has proposed a further wholesale reduction in jury trials. It would abolish the right to elect trial by jury for what are termed 'either way offences' – ie those offences, like theft, where an accused may elect either Crown Court trial or 'summary' trial before magistrates. On present statistics, such a change would remove the right to trial by jury from some 25,000 persons annually.

The Arguments

Debates over the merits of jury trial have continued for many years. So, what are the main pro's and con's?

In favour of jury trials it is often argued that:

(i) they are independent and introduce an element of community justice into the legal system. An accused's guilt or innocence is determined according to the people's standards of behaviour rather than the state's;

(ii) jurors are not privy to evidence excluded by the judge which is too unreliable to be used. In non-jury trials judges have to perform mental gymnastics to try to disregard any evidence that they have decided to exclude;

(iii) Arguments about the quality of jury decision-making underestimate the extent to which questions of guilt or innocence are inevitably value-laden. There is little to indicate that replacing the jury with judicial decision-making would necessarily result in a more rational or accurate system of justice.

On the other hand, it is also pointed out that:

(i) juries are potentially more fallible than the professionals. Research in both England and the USA shows that juries may often encounter difficulties in understanding the evidential issues and the law, and that this can affect their capacity to give a proper verdict. It thus leaves open the possibility that individuals are convicted/acquitted by virtue of prejudice or discrimination, rather than evidence. Research conducted by John Baldwin and Mike McConville in the 1970's concluded that 36% of jury acquittals and 5% of convictionswere questionable on the law or evidence as presented;

(ii) Perhaps connected to the above point, it is also arguable that the capacity of a jury to impose its own values on the case is not such a good thing, if it results in verdicts that are legally unsustainable or 'perverse'. Research suggests that, in fact, very few jury decisions go so far against the weight of evidence as to be perverse, but it might still be argued that the perversity of juries puts the law seriously into disrepute. (*Query: is this automatically a bad thing? If the law is out of step with community feeling, which is wrong – the law or the community?*)

(iii) the presence of a jury cannot overcome other failings in the system – eg if important evidence does not come to light, or unreliable evidence is wrongly admitted by the judge,or the judge gives a highly prejudicial summing-up, a jury is likely to be influenced by such distortions. The **Birmingham Six**, **Guildford Four** and **Cardiff Three**, for example,were all convicted by a jury.

You may feel that the arguments, ultimately, are quite finely balanced, or you may not; there is no absolute answer. If you cannot make up your mind, perhaps you should start by thinking about the values which you think the criminal justice system should serve. How far does the principle of jury trial support or negate those values?

☐ ACCESS TO JUSTICE – THE CASE OF CIVIL LEGAL AID

Legal aid provides the main system of publicly-funded legal services in Britain. It is a mechanism whereby the state will pay the legal fees, or a proportion of those fees, in cases where the client cannot afford to meet the costs of legal action from his or her own resources. Legal aid is available in both civil and criminal cases, though the criteria differ somewhat between the civil and criminal schemes.

Lately, the provision of civil legal aid has been an area of some concern in both the legal and national press; and the current debate raises once again the essential question: what price access to justice?

A brief history of the scheme

The modern civil legal aid scheme was established by the Legal Aid and Advice Act 1948, which was itself based on proposals put forward by the government-appointed *Departmental Committee on Legal Aid and Advice (1945)* – the so-called *Rushcliffe Committee*. The *Rushcliffe Report* is best seen as part of the immediate post-war movement towards a Welfare State. It proposed that legal aid should be made available not only to the poor but also to those of 'small or moderate means'. It envisaged a dual system of support whereby legal aid would be available from both a national, salaried, legal advice service, and from practitioners in private practice. In fact, only the latter form of provision was incorporated in the 1948 Act.

Substantial reforms to the scheme were enacted in 1972, 1979 and again in 1988, but the basic principles have remained remarkably constant. Today, the civil legal aid scheme provides three kinds of assistance:

– legal aid in those cases where court action is anticipated or required;

– advice and assistance under the '*Green Form Scheme*', where the case requires legal work, short of representation before a court;

– assistance by way of representation (ABWOR) under the Green Form Scheme – whereby, exceptionally, costs of representation in proceedings before certain specialist tribunals can be met out of the scheme.

Who is Eligible?

The principle of eligibility enshrined in the 1948 Legal Aid Act, and in operation to this day (more or less), is that assistance should be made available according to the means of the client and the merits of the case. The 'merits test' has not proved particularly problematic; it is a very basic filtering device which serves only to cut-out the clearly hopeless cases which would have no real chance of success if they came to trial. The 'means test' has proven more problematic.This has worked on two principles. First, clients who satisfy a 'poverty line' criterion (normally determined by eligibility to certain social security benefits) are entitled to free legal aid and advice. Second, in other cases, the client will be expected to pay a contribution towards the costs of litigation/advice and assistance according to a 'tariff' – ie, so that as income rises, so to does the person's contribution, until a point is reached where the client will be ineligible under the Scheme, and liable for the costs of all work undertaken.

Eligibility has long been subjected to contradictory pressures. On the one hand, the basic principles of access to justice demand fairly generous eligibility criteria, at least if the scheme is to assist anyone other than the poorest citizens. On the other, there have been almost constant pressures from the Treasury to contain public expenditure, and this has occurred in the context of steady, real, growth in earnings (especially within the middle classes) and an increased demand for legal services.

The result has been that levels of entitlement over the last forty years have undergone something of a roller-coaster ride. In 1950, when the scheme was established, 80% of the population were eligible on income grounds. By 1973 this had halved to 40%, largely because of the failure to update eligibility rates. In 1979, the Labour government substantially increased eligibility rates, back up to 79% of the population; however, by 1990, research was suggesting that eligibility had again slumped to 34%. The result has been a squeezing of the lower and middle income groups in society. In crude terms, the very rich can afford their own lawyers; the very poor get theirs for free; it is the groups in between who may not qualify for legal aid, and not have the private resources to meet the costs themselves.

Even so, expenditure on legal aid represents a not insignificant sum. Figures for 1992/93 show a net cost to taxpayers (for *both* civil and criminal legal aid) of some £900 million. By 1996 total expenditure is anticipated to reach £1.5 billion.

As a result, in recent years, governmental pressure on the Lord Chancellor, Lord Mackay, to limit expenditure has increased markedly. This has been converted into a number of initiatives which have involved: holding down the rates of remuneration paid to lawyers for legal aid work (legal aid is generally significantly less remunerative for lawyers than their private client work);attempts to increase the efficiency/quality of service provided by legal aid practices; and attempts to reduce frauds on the scheme. So far these have not been sufficient, with the result that the government has turned to making real cuts in eligibility criteria.

The 1993 Reforms

A number of substantial changes were introduced in April 1993 which have had the effect of (i) reducing the numbers of people entitled to free legal aid, by a technical adjustment of the means test; (ii) increasing the proportion of disposable income which is payable by clients obliged to make a contribution to their legal aid, and (iii) restricting eligibility to the Green Form Scheme to those clients who are on sufficiently low incomes to claim income support.

The precise effect of these reforms is still difficult to quantify. The changes to legal aid eligibility may not have actually taken anyone right out of the scheme, but it has reduced the numbers entitled to free legal aid by, official estimates suggest, some 127,000. It has also meant that those required to make a contribution to their costs are now likely to pay more than before. How far these changes will deter individuals from seeking legal redress remains to be seen.

The effect of the changes to Green Form entitlement are easier to quantify. The changes to the regulations cut eligibility on income grounds from a maximum of £145 pw disposable income to £61. They have excluded thereby many low income groups, including some on welfare benefits. Estimates suggest that about 150,000 people a year will be taken out of the Green Form Scheme thereby.

The various changes to legal aid have split the legal and political establishments. In 1992, the cross-party House of Commons Home Affairs Committee undertook an emergency inquiry into legal aid; its conclusions were highly critical of the proposed changes. In June 1993, the Law Society (the solicitors' professional body) sued the Lord Chancellor, alleging that the reforms were so contrary to the purposes of the Legal Aid Act 1988 as to be irrational. The Society lost, though it was evident that the judges themselves were less than happy with that outcome. Indeed, we have had an unprecedented split in the ranks of the senior judiciary, with the Lord Chief Justice, Lord Taylor accusing the Lord Chancellor of 'an abdication of responsibility for a large section of those for whom the legal aid system was devised' (The Guardian, 25 May, 1993). Relations between the Legal Aid Board (the organisation actually responsible for administering the Scheme) and the profession also seem to be heading towards an all time low after the vice-president of the Law Society, Charles Elly, reportedly described the Board as 'a downcast institution, riven by internal dissension... gripped by a bunker mentality in which it can trust no-one...' (The Lawyer, 3 May 1994).

The Future

The future, as always, is hard to predict. The Lord Chancellor has promised to restore eligibility levels once economic circumstances permit (New Law Journal, 25 June, 1993), but, understandably perhaps, many in the profession are sceptical. If they are right, and legal aid eligibility continues to fall it will have a number of important ramifications.

First, at a very practical level, it will affect the viability of many of the smaller, particularly inner city law firms, who do not have a sufficient body of private client work to financially support their legal aid practice. This could, in turn have a further negative impact on levels of unmet need for legal advice.

Second, at a more fundamental level, it raises difficult questions about the importance we place on access to justice. How far should we expect the state to fund legal services, so as to provide access? Professors Capelletti and Garth have made the point that 'social justice, as sought by our modern societies, presupposes effective access' (Access to Justice: A World Survey, vol. I, 1978)but if resources are scarce, how do we weigh access to justice against other social benefits, such as health, housing and welfare? Indeed, is it realistically separable from such benefits?

Thirdly, we need to consider, if the capacity or willingness of the state to provide access to justice is limited, to what extent should the legal profession take-on that responsibility? There are a number of possible steps that could be considered here:

(a) practitioners should either financially support or undertake what in America is termed 'pro bono' work. This is work that is undertaken for poorer clients in advice centres, or is supported by private practitioners in return for no fee, or a reduced fee, or payment from a charitable foundation funded by the profession itself. While there is a limited pro bono tradition in England, it is largely underdeveloped. The various options are now beingconsidered by a Law Society Working Group.

(b) The profession could probably do more to encourage litigants to settle disputes by alternative means, such as conciliation or arbitration. More research is needed on civil dispute resolution, but it is certainly arguable that the greater use of less formal dispute mechanisms than the courts could significantly reduce the cost of actions to the legal aid Fund. It might also help speed-up the resolution of cases into the bargain.

(c) Consideration of a 'contingency fee' scheme. This too is an American import, and is commonly described in terms of 'no win – no fee', ie, clients are charged a percentage of any compensation if the case is won, and no fee, or a much lower fee if it is lost. This is a controversial measure. Its supporters argue that it would increase access to the courts,because poorer clients could bring cases without having to worry about who pays the bill at the end. Opponents argue that it will have the reverse effect, because lawyers will not take cases that they do not have an odds-on chance of winning. The debate is likely to run and run, but the Lord Chancellor has already signalled that the door is open, by allowing a conditional fee scheme in personal injury actions. It allows lawyers to forego fees if they loose, but recover up to twice their hourly rate if they win. Again it is too early to say how popular this measure will prove to be, but who knows...

☐ ACCESS TO THE LEGAL PROFESSION

You may have come across some fairly pessimistic warnings about completing your legal training and finding a job. They haven't been included just to put you off, they are based on real facts and statistics.

Going on to be a solicitor

The Policy Studies Institute has recently carried out a survey of 5,000 law students either in their final year at university or their first year of professional legal training. The results are not totally unexpected but still disheartening:

– Applicants for the LPC are at a disadvantage if they attended a New university. About 44% of applicants from Old universities are successful as opposed to just 24% of hopefuls from New universities.

– Applicants looking for training contracts after they finish the LPC face an uphill struggle if:
   (a) they are black or from an ethnic minority. The success rates by race are: whites 47%; Chinese 29%; South Asians 21% and blacks 7%.
   (b) they were educated at a state school and/or a New university. The success rates by institution are: Oxbridge 88%; Old universities 45% and New universities 22%.
   (c) they don't have affluent parents who are in some way connected with the legal profession.

The results of this survey have prompted the Council of Legal Education to make some changes to the system, such as allowing students who fail the LPC to resit the exam automatically and agreeing to set fewer in-course assessments. There has even been a tentative suggestion for UCAS to take over the application process for students looking for training contracts. It is extremely unlikely however that changes within the LPC format and a centralised selection system for articles will be able to remove racism, classism and favouritism from legal training and job hunting.

Going on to be a barrister

The story for budding barristers is no brighter. The Council of Legal Education, which has a monopoly on Bar training, has just changed its selection criteria for accepting students onto the one-year vocational course. They used to operate a system that took degree results into consideration and ran on a first-come-first-served basis. But now the new system ignores degree classification altogether. The selections are now based on:

- a critical reasoning test,
- two application forms, and
- A-level results.

It is this last point which has upset most people. Why should your A-levels have a direct bearing on your admission to Bar training, when the work you've done at university is so much more relevant (and probably of a higher standard)?

The CLE Secretary, Mr John Taylor has defended the selection process on the grounds that all applicants know their A-level results when they apply, but only 28% of applicants know their degree results. And to wait for the degree awards to be available would delay the decisions and 'result in a lot of difficulties for all the students'- even though most law tutors would be able to gauge the degree grades of their students by analysing their university performance.

This set-up has completely ruined the chances of many high calibre students whose A-levels let them down. It is a real kick in the teeth for mature students who are being judged on exams they took 10 or more years ago. Even students who won scholarships from the Inns of Court have been refused. Some of the 1,500 rejected students were so enraged that, at the time of writing, they were about to take the Bar law school to court.

The school has also been criticised by the Barrow inquiry, which unearthed a lot of racial discrimination by chambers. But it has responded to these by making several changes, such as appointing an equal opportunities officer and external examiners, setting up a students' union and introducing a system of double-marking for assessments. Will the selection process have changed by the time you get there? We live in hope...

LORD CHANCELLOR

– The senior member of the legal profession of England and Wales (also Scotland and Northern Ireland).

– A member of the Cabinet.

– Technically he is also Head of the Chancery Division of the High Court (although in practice he never sits) he can also theoretically hear cases which reach the Lords though again rarely does so in practice. The current Lord Chancellor is Lord Mackay who has been criticised by many members of the legal profession over cut-backs in Legal Aid provision.

LORD CHIEF JUSTICE

– The second highest ranking legal position in England after Lord Chancellor.

– LCJ is head of the Criminal Division of the Court of Appeal where he sits. Formally at least he is also head of the Queens Bench Division of the High Court.

– Most of the cases heard by LCJ will be appeals on indictable offences from Crown Court which he will hear with two other judges. The present LCJ is Lord Taylor – formally referred to as Lord Taylor CJ.

MASTER OF THE ROLLS

– The holder of this office is the Head of the Civil Court in England. He sits in the Civil Division of the Court of Appeal.

– Most of the cases he hears are appeals from County Courts on matters like contractual disputes, personal injury, negligence etc.

He will also hear appeals from the High Court on similar matters of greater monetary value, as well as hearing (always with at least two other judges) appeals from the High Court on matters of Chancery dispute, eg, tax, trusts, land, company law, insolvency etc.

– This was the position from which Lord Denning MR became famous (or infamous) for eccentric decisions in the 1960s and 1970s. More recent MRs, however, Lord Donaldson and Sir Thomas Bingham have had a much lower profile, despite the fact that the former was once a strong Tory activist and head of the controversial Industrial Relations Court in the early 1970s.

THE HOUSE OF LORDS

– The Law Lords are officially known as Lords of Appeal in ordinary. They sit on the Cross-benches in the lords and take no part in debates on non-legal matters.

– There are eleven Law Lords in all, including by tradition, two from Scotland. They have all been very senior members of the legal profession and generally today will have been High Court judges followed by a spell in the Court of Appeal.

– Generally the Lords will hear about 50-60 cases each year but only as an appeal court – the final appellate court in England, Wales, Northern Ireland and, for non-criminal cases, Scotland. Because of the great expense of taking a case to the Lords, the majority of cases heard are complex tax questions; corporate disputes etc. Occasionally, however the Lords do hear criminal cases.

COURT OF APPEAL

– These are known as Lord Justices of Appeal. There are 28 in total, most of whom have done a stint in the High Court.

– The Court can hear both Civil and Criminal Appeals, though in practice the majority are appeals on indictment from the Crown Court.

– The present CA is unusual in that it contains a woman – the first ever to sit in the Court. She is Lord Justice Butler-Sloss.

Eyebrows were raised by her appointment in 1987 since she was appointed by the Lord Chancellor only a short time after the previous LC, Lord Havers, had retired. This was convenient since Lord Havers is her elder brother.

HIGH COURT JUDGES

– These are largely civil case judges who sit in the High Court on the Strand. They are known as 'puisne' judges. There are about 80 all told.

– The High Court has three divisions which deal with the following kinds of cases:

(a) Queens Bench Division: mainly contract or tort disputes of high monetary value. Most puisne judges sit here. Also has limited criminal appeal functions.

(b) Family Division: defended divorces, disputed claims over illegitimacy, Children Act 1989 etc. (Has several of that rare breed – female judges).

(c) Chancery Division: taxation of companies, land disputes, insolvency, wills or estates etc. Frequently extremely complex matters of law are involved here and hence expertise of a high order is needed. This division is usually regarded as having the most intellectually gifted judges.

CIRCUIT JUDGES

– These judges sit in the Crown Court or the County Court in one of the six circuits into which England and Wales are divided.

– There are about 300 of them, most of whom have been barristers with at least ten years experience.

– In practice their experiences of major cases are fairly limited since most of the big cases occur in London or the South East circuit.

– Moreover if a Crown Court has to try a serious offence, eg, murder it will be heard by a High Court judge.

RECORDERS

– These are part-time judges of at least five years experience who are appointed to assist circuit judges.

– Interestingly this can be one of the few ways in which solicitors (as opposed to barristers) can become judges. (Certain senior judges have been solicitors at one time, eg, Lord Wilberforce, but they switched to the Bar later in life).

DISTRICT JUDGES

– These are part-time judges who work on civil cases in the local County Court.

– Formally called Registrars, in practice most of their work consists of undefended divorces, Small Claims Arbitration (under £1,000) etc.

MAGISTRATES

– These are lay persons who have no legal qualification. They are thus not judges.

– Their main work is the hearing of summary offences (eg, driving or petty theft). There is no jury in a magistrates court but they may still hear 'either-way' offences with the accused's consent. About 95% of all criminal cases heard in England or Wales begin and end here. All criminal cases must be heard here first even though the more serious cases will be sent to Crown Court.

– They also have a civil jurisdiction, mainly in domestic matters, eg, Children Acts disputes, domestic violence injunctions, juveniles, licensing etc.

ATTORNEY-GENERAL

– This is the government's legal officer. His main job is to represent the Crown in any prosecution involving national security, state secrets and so on. He can also defend for the Crown but rarely does so in practice.

- He is always an MP and usually has substantial experience of legal practice. The current A-G is Nicholas Lyell – presently in hot water for his part in withholding documents in the Matrix-Churchill affair.

OUTLINE OF COURT STRUCTURE

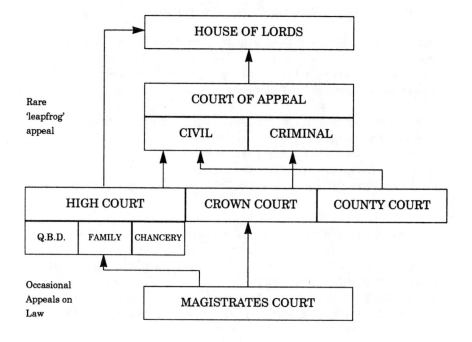

APPENDIX C
SPECIMEN INTERVIEW QUESTIONS

(to be read in conjunction with chapter 5)

Expect the unexpected! Questions may be straightforward and specific, but they can range to the vague and border on the seemingly irrelevant. Be prepared for more than the blindingly obvious, 'Why do you want to study law?' question.

– Have you spoken to any lawyers about their work? Have you visited any courts?
– What makes a good judge/ barrister/ solicitor?
– What area of law are you interested in?
– What is the difference between the Law of Contract and the Law of Tort?

– Have you read about any cases recently?
– Should cannabis/ euthanasia be legalised?
– How do you view Lord Woolf's proposals for a 'shake-up' regarding self-representation in court?
– Should the Child Support Agency change its approach?
– What are the pro's and con's of fusing the two branches of the legal profession?
– Should the police in this country be armed?
– If you were in a position of power, would you change the current civil legal aid situation?
– Should the police spend their time enforcing the laws concerned with begging?
– Why are some juvenile offenders 'sent on holiday'?
– Does the American public have the right to pass judgement on the sentencing of James Bulger's killers?
– Should Britain or any other country intervene in situations like Bosnia/ Somalia/ Rwanda?
– What are your views on the right to silence?
– How can you quantify compensation for victims of crime?
– Should criminals be allowed to sell their stories as 'exclusives'?

- Should the British National Party be allowed to demonstrate with police protection?
- Is it 'barbaric' to cane someone for vandalising cars?

- How does the law affect your daily life?
- What would happen if there were no law?
- Is it really necessary for the law to be entrenched in archaic tradition, ritual and jargon?
- How are law and morality related?
- Does the Church have any impact on law thesedays?
- Do you believe that all people have equal access to justice?
- What is justice?
- Why do we send criminals to prison? What are the alternatives?
- Should the media be more careful with the way in which they report real crime?
- Is law the best way to handle situations like domestic violence/ child abuse/ rape?
- Should British law encompass the laws of ethnic minorities since this society is so multi-cultural?
- What in your opinion are the causes of the increased crime rate?
- Should trial by jury be more or less common?
- Do you think capital punishment should be reinstated?
- Would the law in this country be any different if there was no Royal family?

- You are driving along a busy road with the window down, when a swarm of bees flies into your car. You panic and lose control of the car causing a huge pile-up. Are you legally responsible?
- A blind person, travelling by train, gets out at his/her destination. Unfortunately the platform is shorter than the train, and the blind person falls on to the ground, sustaining several injuries. Who if anyone, can compensate him/her?

APPENDIX D
EMPLOYERS' VIEWS

In this section we give information on the recruiting practices of four legal firms.

Law firm **Cameron, Markby, Hewitt** has absolutely no preference for degree subject when it comes to recruiting trainee solicitors and does not operate any quota in favour of law graduates. They simply want 'the best of the best'. Nor do they recruit from any favoured institutions. However, they do look for a 2:1 and (this year at least) AAB grades at A-level. Applications are welcome from any students likely to meet the academic criteria.

They take part in the early spring milkround and in careers fairs but have made a conscious decision not to participate in the autumn legal milkround as most of their recruitment is carried out over the summer. During the spring term, they give presentations and explain their vacation placement scheme (of two weeks at Easter or three in the summer) to second year law students and third year non-law students as they have found that students who have undertaken a vacation placement make more committed applicants ('it allows for a test on both sides'). Law students may then apply formally over the summer immediately prior to commencing their final year.

Rather than encouraging students to undertake placements at similarly sized City firms, they would like to see students under-taking placements with different sized firms, perhaps one large, one small and possibly one outside London. This would be seen as a positive step. Students would have been able to make comparisons between the firms and would have valid reasons for choosing to apply to Cameron Markby Hewitt.

September 1994 starting salary – £18,000 per annum.

Allen & Overy fills approximately two thirds of its trainee solicitor places with law graduates and one third with students from other disciplines. This broadly reflects the ratio of law to non-law applicants and there is also a matter of cost. The firm sponsors all students through the LPC whether they are lawyers who require only one year's study or non-lawyers who have to complete the CPE as well. Recent successful applicants have had degrees in English, philosophy, history and languages. All subjects are welcome however.

Proven mental ability (demonstrated by at least a 2.1) and personality are more important than subject discipline – as is stamina. One of the partners points out that to work 16 hour days for several days continuously is not uncommon in City law firms. Applicants must appreciate this and must have taken steps to find out how City work differs from that in the provinces. Vacation placements are seen as useful, but since obtaining one of these is almost as competitive as getting articles there is no discrimination against students who have not done one. Work experience of **some** kind, preferably in a financial environment, is seen as useful.

Although 40 per cent of their successful applicants come from Oxbridge, the firm recruits from all institutions including US and EU universities and former polytechnics. Nottingham Trent University, the former Trent Poly, together with Bristol, Durham and London Universities supply good numbers. The firm sees this as due to the fact that these institutions have a tradition of dealing with Allen & Overy. Previous students, currently trainees, feed back positive information.

Allen & Overy take part in careers fairs but visit a limited number of universities on the milk round – Oxford, Cambridge, Bristol and York (the latter for non-law students). The milk round has become less important since many students now apply in advance of this and prefer to be interviewed at Allen & Overy's London offices.

1994 starting salary – £17,750.

Gouldens recruits at least 12 trainee solicitors each year. Twenty five per cent are non-law graduates. Linguists and scientists are particularly valued. All subjects are acceptable however. Present trainees have degrees in economics, engineering, politics, history, biotechnology, zoology, PPE, modern lanaguages and theology. Their backgrounds are equally diverse since they come from Birmingham, Bristol, Cambridge, Durham, Liverpool, London, Oxford, Reading, Salford and Swansea Universities.

There is no standard or model applicant. The firm looks for individuals.

Macfarlanes recruits around 15 trainee solicitors annually, and accepts students from any discipline, sponsoring them through the CPE year. Any degree subject is acceptable but the firm expects both law and non-law graduates to obtain at least a 2.1 and have good grade A-levels. Languages are an added advantage.

Non-academic qualities are particularly important. The firm looks for broad experience and evidence of achievement. Applicants survive the sift of application forms by providing satisfactory answers to, for example:

'Please state your principal current interests and leisure activities. What do you contribute to these interests and how do you benefit from them?'

'Work experience: from which job did you gain the most and why?'

'In which language is your knowledge: fluent; good; adequate; basic?'

Interviews are conducted in London, and if there is sufficient demand, at Birmingham, Bristol, Cambridge, Durham, Exeter, Nottingham, Oxford, Southampton and Warwick Universities.

Starting salary – £18,000.

APPENDIX E
GLOSSARY OF TERMS

ADMINISTRATIVE LAW: This is one of the core (or exemption) courses needed for a qualifying law degree. It usually teams up with Constitutional Law. And it looks at the legal position of the government, public and local authorities and others who wield some kind of power over broadly defined policy, such as town planning, public health and the like.

ARTICLES: The outdated name given to the two years after an LPC when you train as a kind of apprentice solicitor. Now called 'training contract'. In some cases, you can reduce the time spent on articles by completing work placements as part of an undergraduate degree. But even then they last a minimum of one and a half years.

BLACK LETTER LAW: Means the fundamental areas of law like Law of Contract and Equity and Trusts. Doesn't include the more obscure or ephemeral law courses such as Feminist Perpectives in Law or Philosophy of Law. Tends only to examine law found in the law reports and statute books.

CATS (Credit Accumulation and Transfer Scheme): An increasing number of degree programmes are being broken down into units and a certain number of credits are allotted for each successfully completed unit. The advantage to this is that students can now switch from full-to part-time study, or even from one university to another much more smoothly without affecting their total number of credits. It also allows students to take time off their degree should they need to, and their studies are just put on ice, so no separate unit of study is ever lost or wasted.

CD-ROM: Literally, Compact Disk Read Only Memory. These represent a wealth of knowledge at your fingertips. The CDs are used to store vast amounts of information (written, visual or audio) that you can call up on a computer. You're likely to find that schools and universities are better stocked with CD-ROMs than many businesses!

CIVIL LAW: Unfortunately has several meanings. Can refer to Roman Law but it is more likely to mean either, (a) Private Law ie all law other than Criminal, Administrative, Military and Church Law, or (b) the system of law which grew from Roman Law as opposed to the English system of Common Law.

CLEARING: The process that runs throughout September when students without places at university apply for the remaining degree programmes. A list of the available institutions and courses is published at the beginning of September.

CLINICAL LEGAL EDUCATION: This is the opportunity for you to get some hands-on experience with real life cases without being able to go hideously wrong. Students, under supervision from qualified practitioners, give free legal advice to clients and usually see a case right through from beginning to end.

COMETT: This is one of the European programmes that enable students to travel to various parts of Europe either to study or to get onto work placements. Only good-will and academic links are guaranteed – you may have to find your own funding. Comett focuses on placements and technology. And other programmes in the same family include Erasmus, Lingua (language oriented) and Tempest (East Europe).

COMMON LAW: This started about a thousand years ago in Britain. Up until then, each locality had its own customs and practices for dealing with problems and misdemeanours. So, Common Law was an attempt to iron out inconsistencies between different areas (basically so the men at the top could ensure their incomes and maintain their power) by applying one set of rules to similar circumstances.

COMMON PROFESSIONAL EXAMINATION (CPE): This is the one year course that non-law graduates must take to get onto the Legal Practice Course, on the road to becoming a solicitor. It costs between £2,500 and £6,500. You can avoid it by making sure you fit all the six core courses into your law degree.

CONSTITUTIONAL LAW: The rules that control what the Crown, judiciary, Parliament and government do in relation to the country and all the individuals within it. But the Constitution of the UK remains largely unwritten, unlike most other states and comprises statutes, Common Law rules and Constitutional Conventions.

CONTRACT LAW (LAW OF CONTRACT): There is an area of overlap between the Laws of Tort and Contract. The same set of circumstances can even lead to tortious or contractual actions, so look up Tort as well. Also, get used to this sort of far fetched question: Adam has a TV which he promises to sell to Brian. Before he gets the telly though, Brian arranges to sell it to Chris for a tidy profit. But Adam changes his mind about the deal and sells it to David instead. When David receives the TV, it has badly damaged in transit so he calls Adam to complain. Adam directs David to the small print at the bottom of the receipt that passes all responsibility onto the haulier, and so on... Who owns the TV and who should pay for the repairs? Yes, this is the kind of thing that tutors dream up to antagonise their students. It is an example of the Law covering contracts ie legally binding agreements (written, verbal or even implied) between two or more parties coming about as a result of offer and acceptance although there are several other criteria that must be fulfilled too.

CORE SUBJECTS: Currently these are Constitutional and Administrative Law; Contract and Tort; Criminal Law; Equity and Trusts and Property Law. They make up a qualifying law degree that will exempt you from the CPE course after you graduate. Another subject, the Law of the EC will soon be added to this list.

CPE: See Common Professional Examination

CPS: See Crown Prosecution Service

CRIMINAL LAW: One of the cores. Crime is so often sensationalised that Criminal Law needs little introduction but a lot of explanation since the media continually obscure the legal points with hype. The Law basically defines those acts that are seen to be public wrongs and are therefore punishable by the state. Most crimes are made up of two elements – the act itself (*actus reus*) and the thinking behind it (the mens rea), both of which must be proved 'beyond reasonable doubt' in court to establish guilt.

CROWN PROSECUTION SERVICE (CPS): Born in 1986, the CPS, headed by the Director of Public Prosecutions, is responsible for virtually all the criminal proceedings brought in by the police in England and Wales, although the lawyers within the CPS don't always bring a case to court.

DEGREE CLASSIFICATION: Degrees are broken down into several different groups: First Class Honours; Upper Second Class Honours (or 2:1); Lower Second Class Honours (or 2:2); Third Class Honours and Pass. To get a place on an LPC, students, on paper, need a Second Class Honours degree or better, but in practice, even a 2:2 isn't necessarily good enough anymore.

DELICT (LAW OF DELICT): Simply the Scottish name for Tort.

DPP: Director of Public Prosecutions. See Crown Prosecution Service.

EC: European Community – what else?

EQUITY: Half of the double act Equity and Trusts and one of the exemption courses. It is a (still developing) body of legal principles. And it originated in the Middle Ages when, if you felt the Common Law was letting you down, you could petition the king's Chancellor for a fair appraisal of the situation. The Chancellor was keen to see justice done and wasn't too bothered about the rigidity of the Law. Even now, Equity prevails over the rules of Law, but the system of Equity is no longer as arbitrary as before. The main areas of Equity cover trusts, property and remedies (eg injunctions). Look up the 'Anton Piller' order which is a more recent example of Equity at work.

ERASMUS: See Comett

EVIDENCE: Remember that Tom Hanks film where the plot hinges on whether or not it's OK to use a crucial piece of evidence in court? Well, he lied in 'The Bonfire of the Vanities', and it was the Law of Evidence that he broke. This Law covers the presentation of facts and proof in court. It is often associated with hearsay evidence which isn't always admissible, but also covers topics like confessions and the credibility of witnesses.

EXEMPTION SUBJECTS: See Core Subjects

FRESHERS: First Year students.

HEFCE: The Higher Education Funding Council of England is currently carrying out a survey of law courses at universities around the country. They are particularly interested in the teaching and learning standards and are awarding universities grades based on a three point scale, namely, 'excellent', 'satisfactory' and 'unsatisfactory'. Their report should be ready by summer 1994 and you can get hold of a copy for £2 from the Quality Assessment Division, HEFCE, Northavon House, Coldharbour Lane, Bristol BS16 1QD.

HONOURS: See Degree Classification

IT: Not the scary movie, but just the abbreviation for Information Technology, that's to say, the use of computers and networks for easy storage, retrieval and communication of information.

JANET: Stands for Joint Academic NETwork, and she connects students at various universities around the country by computer.

JURISPRUDENCE: This is essentially the philosophy and theories of Law. Jurisprudence units get right down to grass roots level and usually examine Law from a number of angles, such as Natural Law, Marxism and the Critical School.

JUSTIS: This is a legal database giving you access to Law related information on computer. It is very similar to Lexis and Lawtel.

LAND LAW (PROPERTY LAW): No points for guessing that this looks at who has rights (equitable and real) in different types of property and how these rights or responsilibities may be established or transferred. It covers subjects like mortgages, trusts, landlords and tenants, leases, easements and covenants.

LAW SCHOOL: Simply refers to the Law Departments within universities. Not to be confused with College of Law where students study their LPC.

LAWTEL: See Justis

LEXIS: See Justis

LINGUA: See Comett

LPC: Legal Practice Course – the relatively new vocational one-year course after graduation (with a qualifying degree) and prior to the two-year training contract, designed for intending solicitors.

MILKROUND: This is the slang term for the visits that potential employers make to the universities in order to attract and interview potential recruits. They usually inform the university careers office, advertise in the student press and book a conference suite at a local hotel where they lay on refreshments and interviews.

MODULAR DEGREES: Some universities have reduced their degrees to modules – the building blocks of individualistic (and sometimes directionless) courses. Modular degrees enable you to create a degree around your own interests subject to timetabling, but since most Law students want to take the core courses within their degrees anyway, this added flexibility doesn't necessarily add a very exciting new dimension to university life.

MOOT: This is a mock court room trial. Some universities have specially made rooms for that really authentic feel, and others even go as far as to include video cameras to record your performance! But on the whole, moots are organised as extra-curricular/optional activities to improve your confidence and help develop your legal skills of presenting a clear, logical argument and questioning a witness.

OBLIGATIONS (LAW OF OBLIGATIONS): This is just another name for the Laws of Tort and Contract.

OPEN DAYS: Go to them! Not that many Law Schools invite potential students to interview thesedays, so Open Days are the best chance you have to see the Law Department, quiz the Law tutors and get the inside story from the students who are already there. Don't just walk around the campus like a sheep, make the effort to do some groundwork before you go so you can ask something worthwhile when you get there.

PRIVATE LAW: These are those bits of the Law that are concerned with the relations between individuals that really have nothing to do with the state, but that doesn't stop the state intervening in certain circumstances of course. The areas are Family Law, Property Law and Trusts, Contract and Tort.

PROPERTY LAW: See Land Law

PUBLIC LAW: Sometimes this is the core course Constitutional and Administrative thinly disguised.

Although strictly speaking, Public Law also includes areas like Tax Law and Criminal Law since they too are concerned with the relationship between the state and its individuals.

SEMESTER: Typically 15 weeks. Many universities are changing their systems in line with their European neighbours and converting the academic year to two semesters (no you won't miss out on Christmas or Easter holidays). The first one starts in September or October and finishes in February and then the second one starts in February and goes on until June. They are usually made up of 12 weeks teaching and three weeks of exams or assessments, as many subjects are only timetabled for one semester and need to be examined as soon after they've finished as possible.

STATUTE: A general word for a law passed by parliament

STATUTE BOOK: The list of all statutes that are currently in force.

SUBSTANTIVE LAW: Virtually all universities put most of the emphasis on substantive Law at the undergraduate level. It is simply that huge part of the Law that deals with duties and rights and everything else that does not fall into the category of practice and procedure.

TEMPEST: See Comett

TORT: Imagine it's a hot August day. You're gasping for a drink so you go into a cafe with your friend who buys you a bottle of beer. As you refill your glass you spot something a little suspicious and on closer inspection realise it's the decomposed remains of a snail! Do you...
(a) Drink the beer?
(b) Tell your friend to ask for a refund?

(c) Kick up a real furore and bring an action in tort against the manufacturer for negligence in production causing you to suffer shock and an upset stomach?

If your name was Mrs Donoghue and the year was 1928 then you'd go for option (c) and win the case marking a milestone for the tort of negligence in English Law! These days, torts often make headline news (eg Hillsborough). They are largely concerned with providing compensation for people who have been wronged and suffered personal injury or damage to their property through negligence, defamation, nuisance, intimidation etc.

TRUSTS: See Equity. Taking the simplistic approach, trusts arise when someone transfers property to you but you can't use it. This is because the property is held on your behalf by trustees until you're 18. The property is entrusted to these trustees until you are able to choose to dissolve the trust and look after – or spend – the property yourself.

VOCATIONAL LAW COURSES: Turn back to the beginning of Chapter 3 where you'll find definitions of the types of law courses available.

FURTHER READING

General Books on Law:

There are a number of good introductory texts on English Law and the processes of learning the law. Among the ones we would recommend are:

P. Harris, *'An Introduction to Law'*, 4th edition, London: Butterworths, 1993.

J.A. Holland & J.S. Webb, *'Learning Legal Rules'*, 2nd edition, London: Blackstone Press,1993.

S. Lee & M. Fox, *'Learning Legal Skills'*, London: Blackstone Press, 1991.

Miscarriages of Justice:

P. Hill & M. Young, *'More Rough Justice'*, London, Penguin, 1986.

M. Mansfield, *'Presumed Guilty: The British Legal System Exposed'*, London: Heinemann,1993.

Runciman Commission, *'Report of the Royal Commission on Criminal Justice'*, London: HMSO, 1993.

C. Walker & K. Starmer (eds), *'Justice in Error'*, London: Blackstone Press, 1993.

Trial by Jury:

J. Baldwin & M. McConville, *'Jury Trials'*, Oxford: Oxford University Press, 1979.

C. Walker & K. Starmer (eds), *'Justice in Error'*, London: Blackstone Press, 1993.

M. Zander, *'A Matter of Justice'*, Oxford: Oxford University Press, 1989.

Civil Legal Aid:

Most of the information cited in this section is too recent to have found its way into the textbooks, and has been gathered from national newspapers and the academic press; other useful sources of information on legal aid and unmet need, include:

S.H. Bailey & M.J. Gunn, *'Smith & Bailey on the Modern English Legal System'*, London: Sweet & Maxwell, 1991

P.A. Thomas (ed) *'Tomorrow's Lawyers'*, Oxford: Blackwell, 1992.

General Books on Higher Education:

Brian Heap, *'The Complete Degree Course Offers for Entry into Higher Education 1995'*, 25th edition, Trotman, 1994.

Brian Heap, *'How to Choose Your Degree Course'*, 4th edition, Trotman, 1994.

Tony Higgins and Stephen Lamley, *'How to Complete Your UCAS Form 1995 Entry'*, Trotman, 1994.

'Getting into University and College', 2nd edition, Trotman, 1994.

MPW, *'Getting into Oxford and Cambridge'*, 4th edition, Trotman, 1994.

Klaus Boehm and Jenny Lees-Spalding (editors), *'The Student Book 1995'*, 1994.

'The Time Out/NUS Student Guide', Bloomsbury, 1991.

'Mature Students Guide', Trotman, 1994.

'The Alternative Guide to the Sixth Form', 1994.

'University and College Entrance – the Official Guide '95', UCAS, 1994.

'The UCAS Handbook', UCAS, 1994.

'Entrance Guide to Higher Education in Scotland', Committee of Scottish Higher Education Principals.

'The Potter Guide to Higher Education', Dalebank Books.

'Sponsorships', Careers and Occupational Information Centre.

'Clearing the Way', Trotman.

'Students' Money Matters', Trotman.

Newspapers, Periodicals

It is important to keep in touch with developments in the law. The law reports of the serious national papers and periodicals such as *The Economist* are a useful source of information.

Other essential books from Trotman's...

The Complete Degree Course Offers 1995
by Brian Heap
25th Edition
This essential book for applicants to higher education includes points requirements for entry to all first degree courses, advice on how to choose a course and institution, information on how to complete the new section 10 on the UCAS form and much more.
Price: £14.95
Published April 1994

How To Choose Your Degree Course
by Brian Heap
4th Edition
The long awaited new edition of this book contains general advice on how to go about choosing which degree subject to study, looking at A-level subjects and their related courses, and at career groups and specific careers.
Price: £11.95
Published April 1994

How To Choose Your Higher National Diploma Course
Second Edition
This extensively revised and updated publication provides information on: entrance requirements, course descriptions, selection criteria and procedures, intake numbers and applications received, sponsorship and work placements, employment statistics as well as information on GNVQs and NVQs.
Price: £14.95

Order Form (please photocopy)

Please send me the following books:

		Qty	Total
Degree Course Offers 1995	£14.95 + 2.20 p+p	_____	£_____
How To Choose Your Degree Course	£11.95 + 2.20 p+p	_____	£_____
How To Choose Your HND Course	£14.95 + 2.20 p+p	_____	£_____
		Total	**£**_____

Please call us on 081-332-2132 for Access and Visa orders and postage and packing rates for multiple copy orders.

Trotman books are available through good bookshops everywhere.

Cash Orders: Please make your cheque payable to **Trotman & Company** and send it to: **12 Hill Rise, Richmond, Surrey, TW10 6UA.**
Credit Orders: only for schools'/organisations' orders of **over £35.** Please attatch your **official order form** to ours. The original invoice will be sent with the books, payment is due within 28 days.

GET IN WITH A GUIDE

Getting into higher education may be the toughest challenge you've yet faced. MPW Guides can help . . .

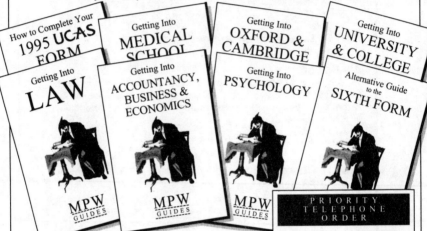

How to Complete Your
1995 **UCAS FORM**

Getting Into
MEDICAL SCHOOL

Getting Into
OXFORD & CAMBRIDGE

Getting Into
UNIVERSITY & COLLEGE

Getting Into
LAW

Getting Into
ACCOUNTANCY, BUSINESS & ECONOMICS

Getting Into
PSYCHOLOGY

Alternative Guide
to the
SIXTH FORM

MPW GUIDES